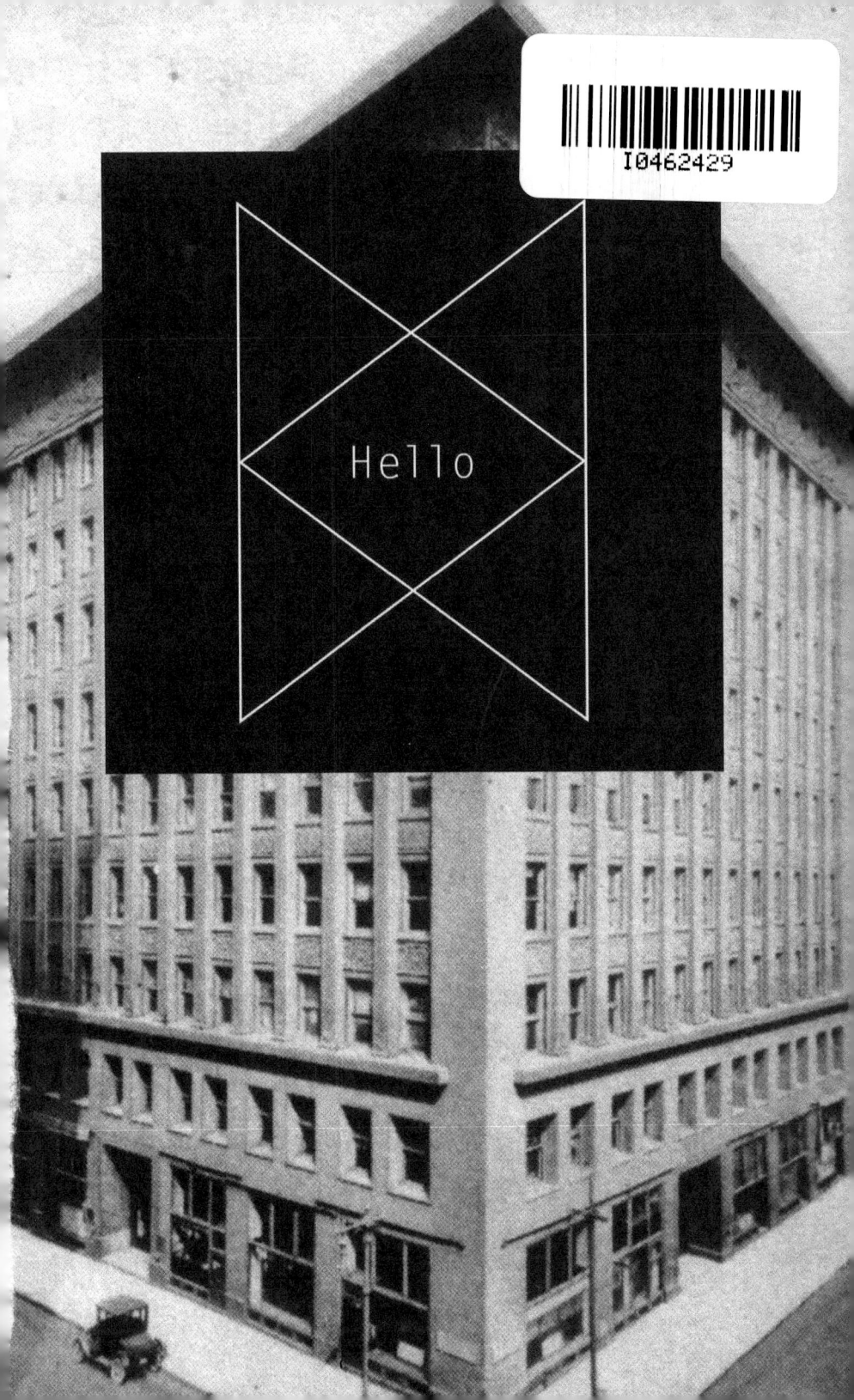

Hello

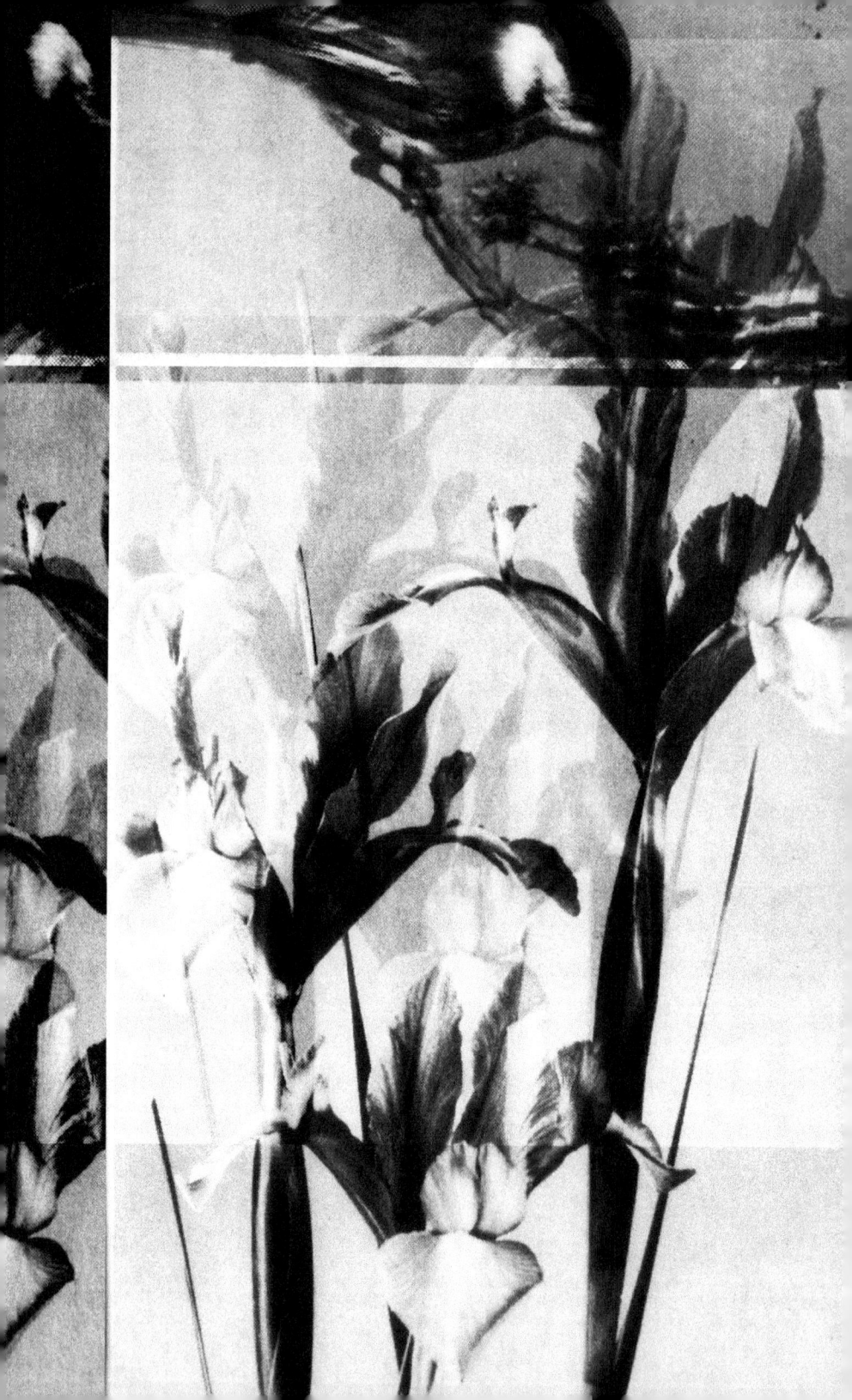

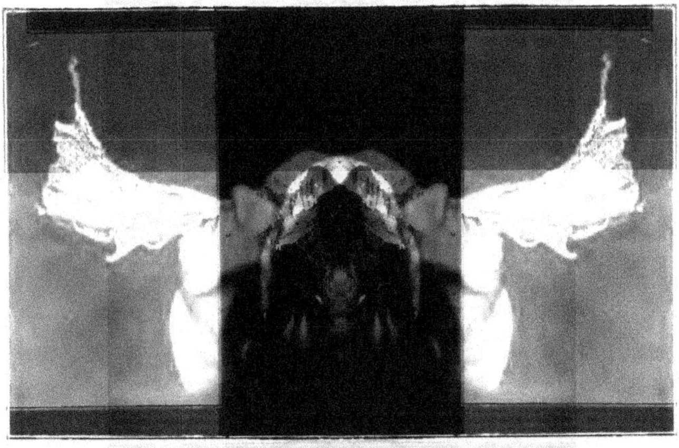

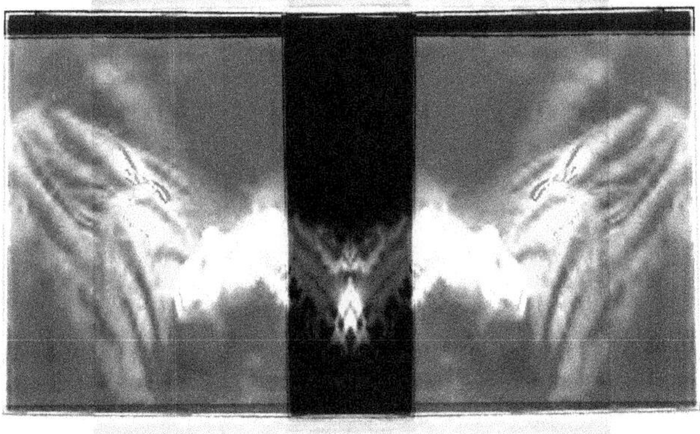

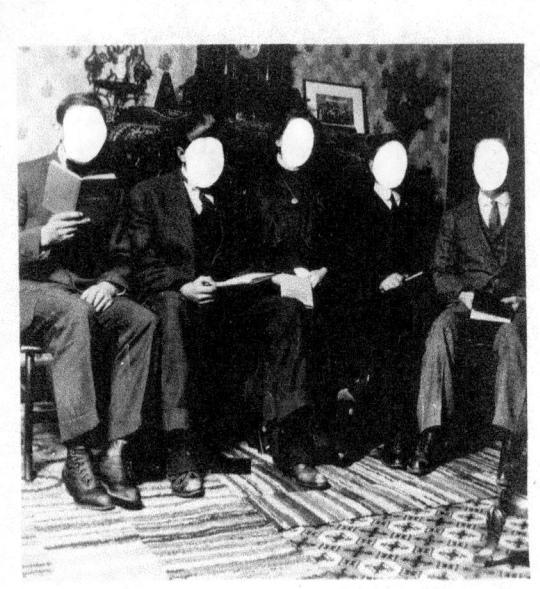

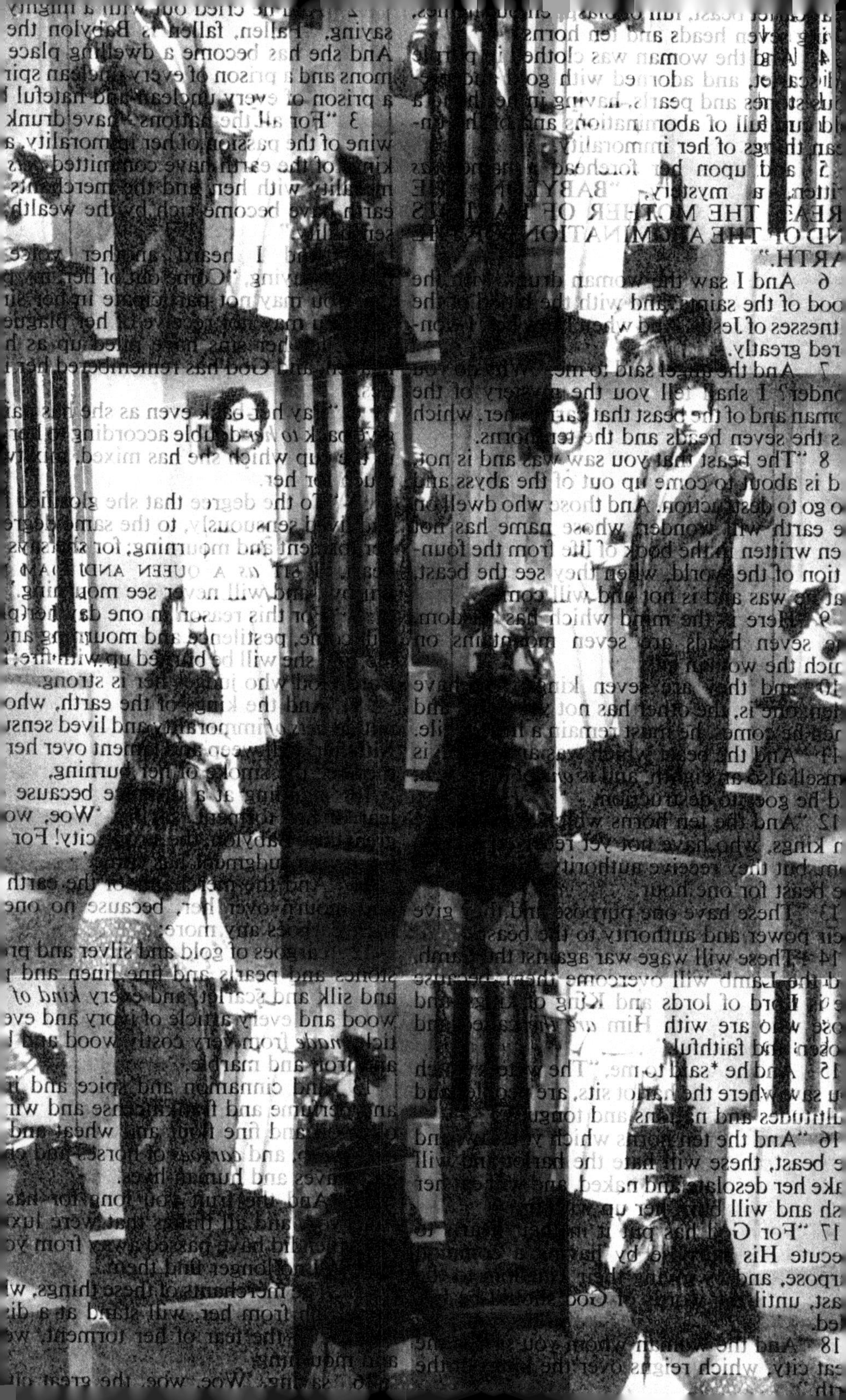
saying, "Fallen, fallen is Babylon the
And she has become a dwelling place
a prison of every unclean and hateful
3 "For all the nations have drunk
wine of the passion of her immorality
earth have become rich by the wealth
heard another voice
from heaven, saying, "Come out of her, my
so that you will not participate in her sins
and God has remembered her
double according to
cup which she has mixed, mix twice
for her.
To the degree that she glorified
and lived sensuously, to the same degre
torment and mourning; for she says
will never see mourning.
For this reason in one day her p
will come, pestilence and mourning an
she will be burned up with fire;
God who judges her is strong.
"And the kings of the earth, who
lived sensu
lament over her
smoke of her burning,
'Woe, wo
city! For
of the earth
over her, because no one
any more;
cargoes of gold and silver and pr
stones and pearls and fine linen and
and silk and scarlet, and every kind of
wood and every article of ivory and eve
iron and marble,
and cinnamon and spice and
and fine flour and wheat and
and human lives.
no longer find them.
merchants of these things, w
from her, will stand at a di
the fear of her torment, we
saying, 'Woe, woe, the great cit
seven heads and ten horns.
4 And the woman was clothed in purple
and scarlet, and adorned with gold and precious
stones and pearls, having in her hand a
gold cup full of abominations and of the unclean things of her immorality,
5 and upon her forehead a name was
written, a mystery, "BABYLON THE
GREAT, THE MOTHER OF HARLOTS
AND OF THE ABOMINATIONS OF THE
EARTH."
6 And I saw the woman drunk with the
blood of the saints, and with the blood of the
witnesses of Jesus. And when I saw her, I won-
dered greatly.
7 And the angel said to me, "Why do you
wonder? I shall tell you the mystery of the
woman and of the beast that carries her, which
has the seven heads and the ten horns.
8 "The beast that you saw was and is not,
and is about to come up out of the abyss and
to go to destruction. And those who dwell on
the earth will wonder, whose name has not
been written in the book of life from the foundation of the world, when they see the beast,
that he was and is not and will come.
9 "Here is the mind which has wisdom.
The seven heads are seven mountains on
which the woman sits,
10 and they are seven kings; five have
fallen, one is, the other has not yet come; and
when he comes, he must remain a little while.
11 "And the beast which was and is not, is
himself also an eighth, and is one of the seven,
and he goes to destruction.
12 "And the ten horns which you saw are
ten kings, who have not yet received a kingdom,
but they receive authority as kings with
the beast for one hour.
13 "These have one purpose and they give
their power and authority to the beast.
14 "These will wage war against the Lamb,
and the Lamb will overcome them, because
He is Lord of lords and King of kings, and
those who are with Him are the called and
chosen and faithful."
15 And he *said to me, "The waters which
you saw where the harlot sits, are peoples and
multitudes and nations and tongues.
16 "And the ten horns which you saw, and
the beast, these will hate the harlot and will
make her desolate and naked, and will eat her
flesh and will burn her up with fire.
17 "For God has put it in their hearts to
execute His purpose by having
purpose, and by giving their kingdom to the
beast, until the words of God should be
fulfilled.
18 "And the woman whom you saw is the
great city, which reigns over the kings of the
earth."

...s beheld them.

in that hour there was a great ... and a tenth of the city fell, ... and people were killed ... and the rest were terrified ... the God of heaven.

second woe ... beast behold ... comes quick...

the seventh angel sounded, and ... loud voices in heaven, say... dom of the world has become the ... Lord and His Christ, and ... forever and ever."

be twenty-four elders, who sat on ... before God, fell on their faces ... God.

thee thanks, ... Lord God the Al... art and who wast, because Thou ... thy great power and hast begun to ...

... enraged ... and Thy ... the dead to ... reward to ... ...servants and to the ... ... Then came, the ... ...who

...emple ... God which is in ... ...ned, and was seen ... His cov-... His te... ... there were ... ...ngs and ... ...d peals of ... an earthquake ... great hail.

...great sign ap... in heaven: ... clothed with the sun, and the ... her feet ... head a crown ...

...s with ... and she cried ... labor and in... to give birth. ...other sign ap...ed in heaven: ...great red d... having seven

saying, ...

"Now salvation, and the power, and the kingdom of our God and the authority of His Christ ... come, for the accuser of our both... real him ... who ...tes them before ... day and n...

...overcame him ... se of the blo... lamb and because of the word of their ... and they did not love their life even t...

...2 ... this reason, rejoice, O heavens and ... who dwell in them. Woe to the earth and ... sea, for the devil has come down to ... having great wrath, knowing that he has ... a short time.

...when ... dragon saw that he was ... down to the earth, ... persecuted the ... who gave ... to the male child. ...the two wings of the great eagle ... to the woman, in order that ... fly into the wilderness to her place, ... she was nourished for a time and times ... time, from the presence of the ser...

...nd the serpent ... water li... of his mouth after the woman, so ... cause her to be swept away with ...

...nd the earth ...ed the woman, ... earth opened its mouth and drank up ... which the dragon poured out of ...

...And the dragon was enraged with ... ...and went off to make war with the ... offspring, who keep the commandm... ...and hold to the testimony of Jesus.

And he stood on the sand of the seash...
And I saw a beast coming up out ... ...the sea, having ten horns and seven heads, ...horns were ten diadems, and on ... ...were blasphemous names ...

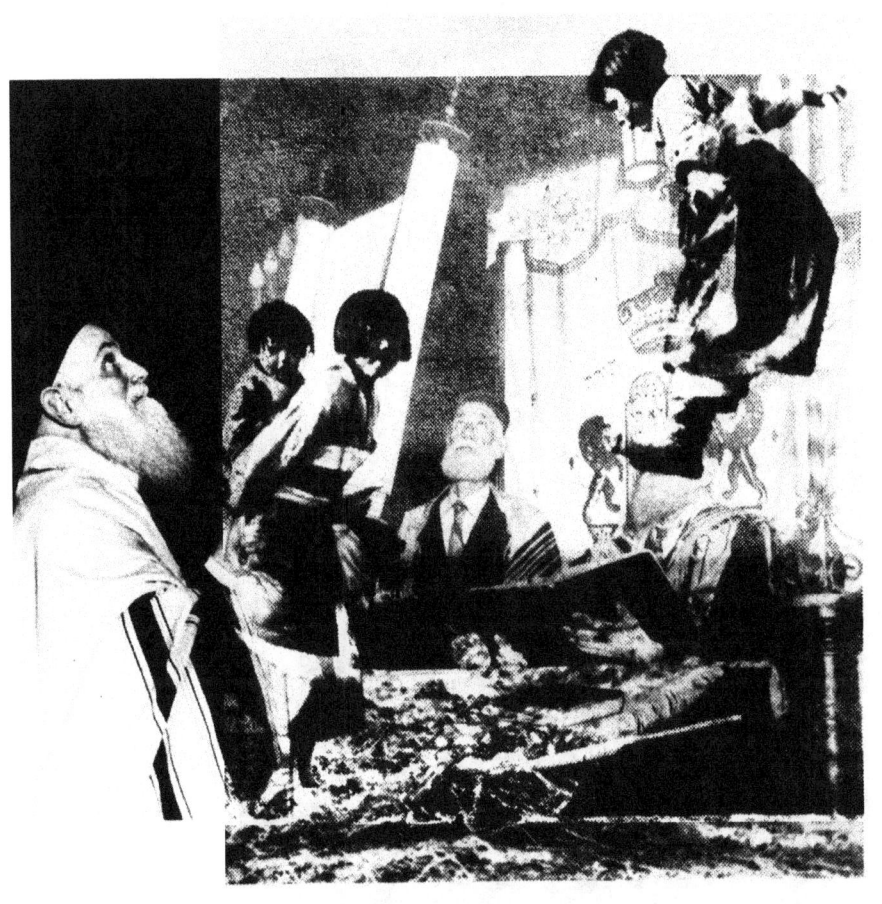

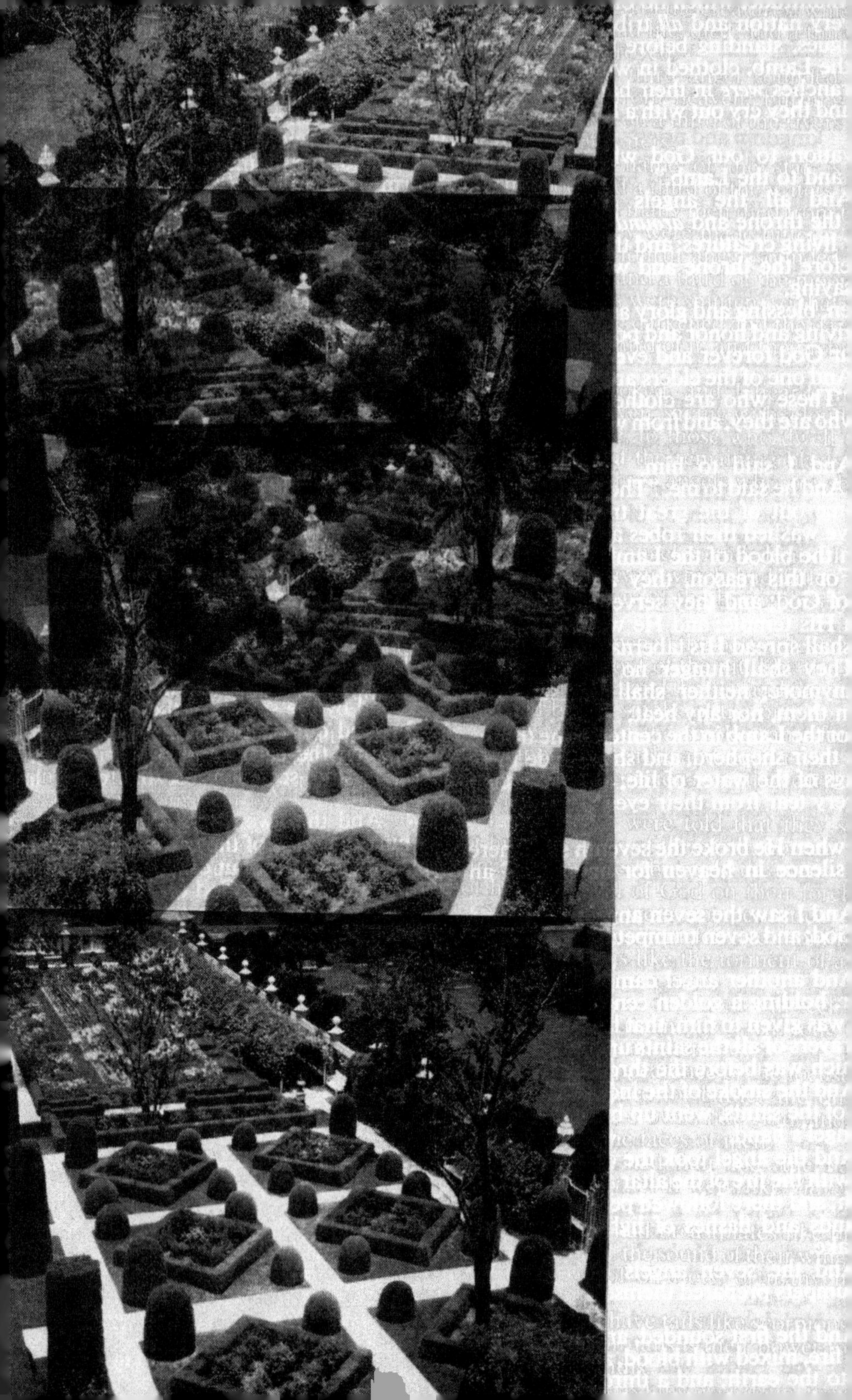
ery nation and of all trib
gues, standing before
he Lamb, clothed in w
ranches were in their h
nd they cry out with a
ation to our God wh
and to the Lamb.
nd all the angels
the throne and arou
living creatures; and t
efore the throne and w
aying,
n, blessing and glory a
giving and honor and po
e God forever and ev
And one of the elders an
These who are clothe
who are they, and from w
And I said to him
And he said to me, Th
washed their robes a
the blood of the Lamb
For this reason, they
of God; and they serve
shall spread His tabern
They shall hunger no
sun beat on them, nor any heat;
the Lamb in the cente
their shepherd, and sh
es of the water of life
when He broke the sev
silence in heaven for
And I saw the seven an
God, and seven trumpe
And another angel cam
holding a golden cen
was given to him muc
And the angel took the

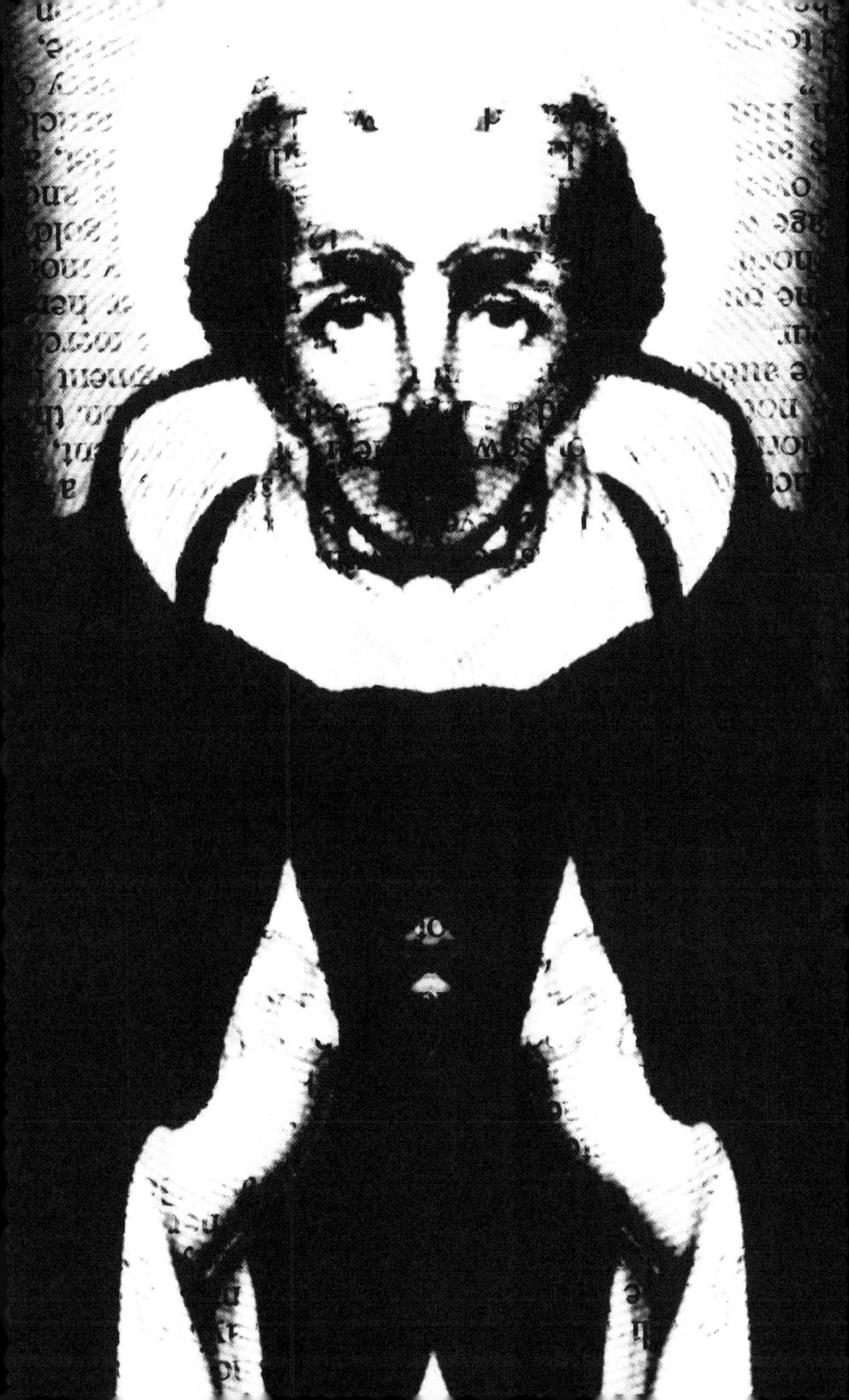

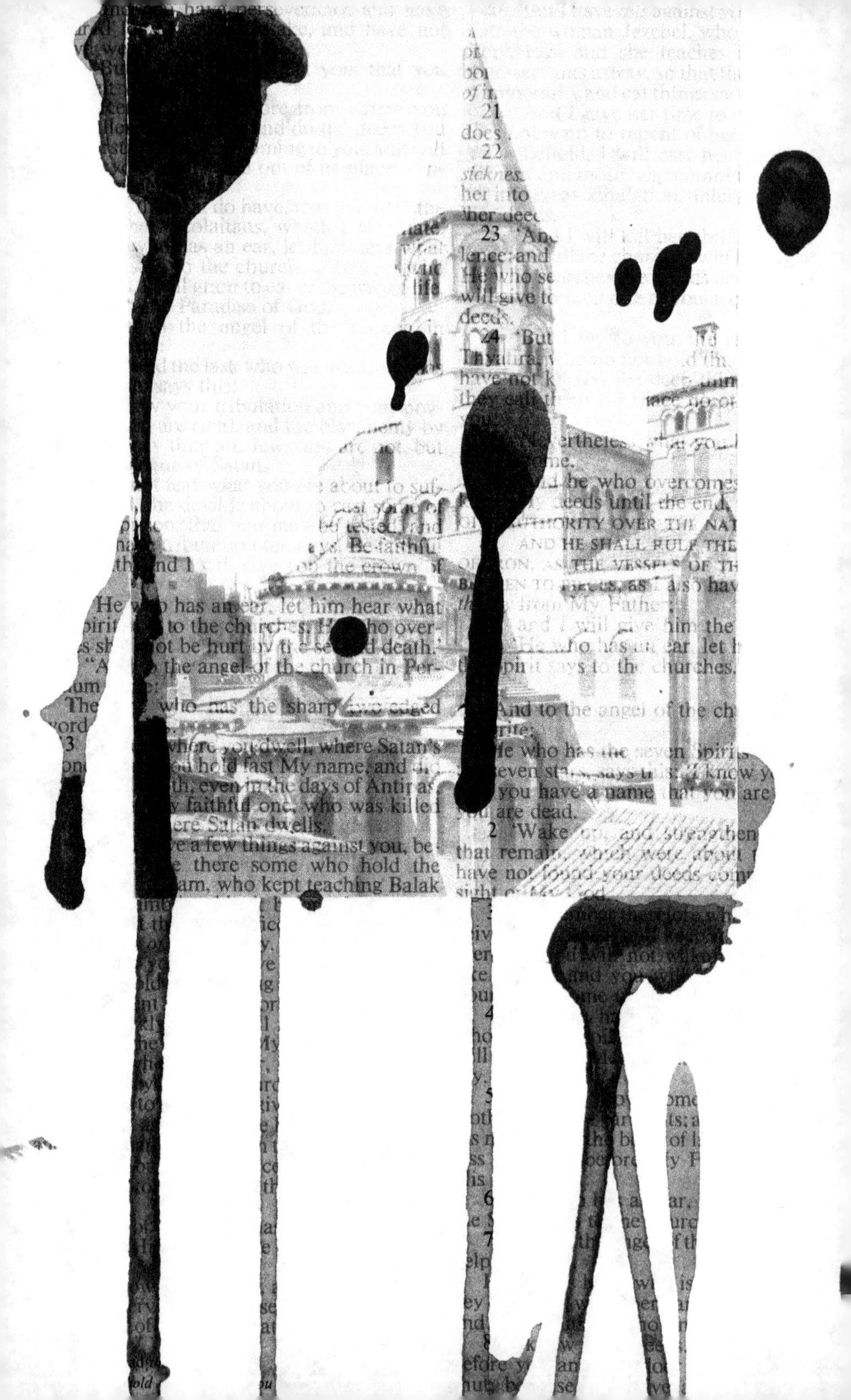

He who has an ear, let him hear what
be hurt by the second death.
the angel of the church in Per-
The who has the sharp two-edged
where you dwell, where Satan's
you hold fast My name, and
even in the days of Antipas,
faithful one, who was killed
where Satan dwells.
a few things against you, be-
there some who hold the
who kept teaching Balak
And he who overcomes
deeds until the end
AUTHORITY OVER THE NAT
AND HE SHALL RULE THE
And to the angel of the ch
He who has the seven Spirits
you have a name that you are
you are dead.
2 'Wake up, and strengthen
that remain, which were about t
have not found your deeds com

...ehold, I will... of Satan, who s... at th... not, but he—beh... I wi... ne and bow down... your... ...e, I have loved y... because you... w... ...nce, I al... ...eeping, ...t... ...l the who... d. to... those who... on the ea...

...fast what... take your... ...l make him a... ...nd he will... ...ll write up... ...e name of the... ...alem, which... My G... ...him hear w... ...he church in...

...d true Witness... n of God, s... you are neith... you were cold o... ...ewarm, and... you out of... ...re rich, and have... ...have need of nothing... ...ow that... are wretched... ...d and nak... Me gold re... ...ome rich, and... ...othe yourself... ...dness may n... point your eye... ...prove and... ...d repent. ...r and knock... ...eas the do...

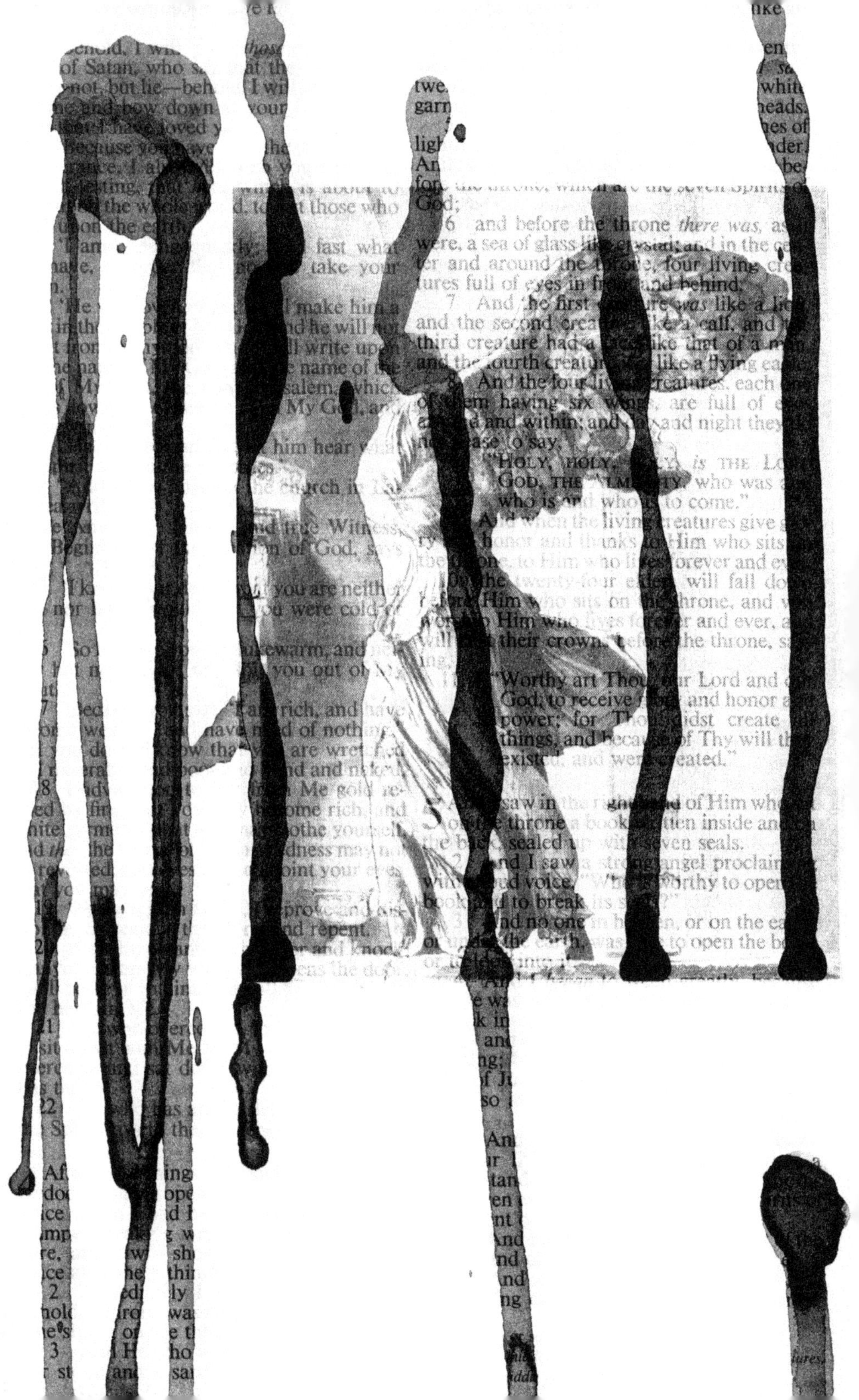

6 and before the throne there was, as... were, a sea of glass like crystal; and in the ce... ter and around the throne, four living cre... tures full of eyes in front and behind.

7 And the first creature was like a lio... and the second creature like a calf, and... third creature had a face like that of a man... and the fourth creature like a flying eag...

8 And the four living creatures, each on... of them having six wings, are full of e... around and within; and day and night they... ...cease to say,

"HOLY, HOLY, HOLY is THE LO... GOD, THE ALMIGHTY who was a... who is and who is to come."

...And when the living creatures give g... ...honor and thanks to Him who sits... ...he throne, to Him who lives forever and e... ...the twenty-four elders will fall do... ...m Him who sits on the throne, and w... ...worship Him who lives forever and ever, a... ...will cast their crowns before the throne, sa...

"Worthy art Thou, our Lord and... God, to receive glory and honor a... power; for Thou didst create... things, and because of Thy will th... existed and were created."

5 And I saw in the right hand of Him who... ...on the throne a book written inside and on... ...the back, sealed up with seven seals.

2 And I saw a strong angel proclaim... with a loud voice, "Who is worthy to open... book and to break its seals?"

...And no one in heaven, or on the ea... ...der the earth was able to open the bo...

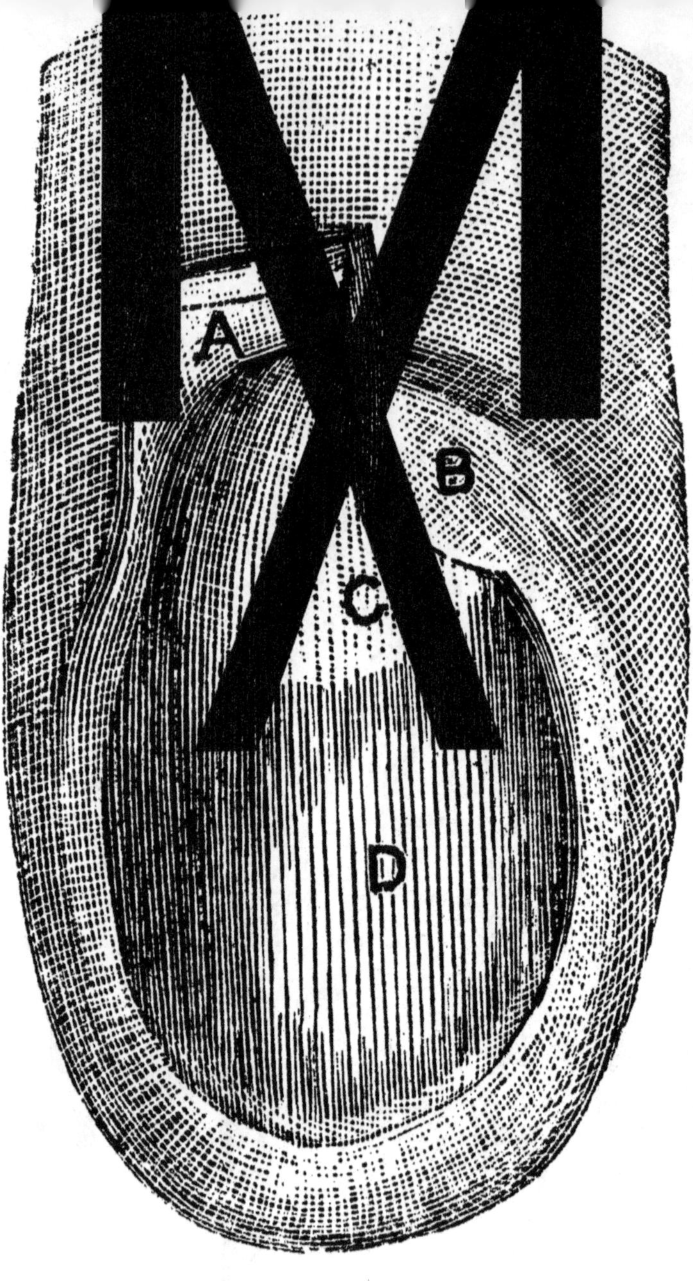

A

B

C

D

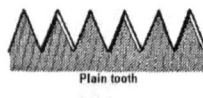
Plain tooth

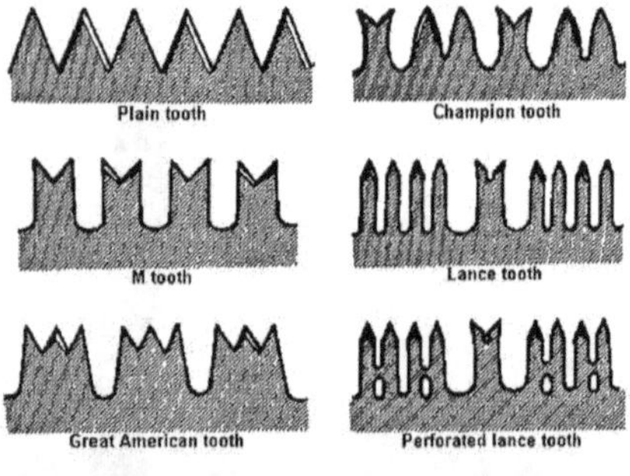

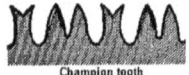
Champion tooth

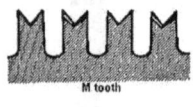
M tooth

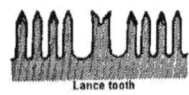
Lance tooth

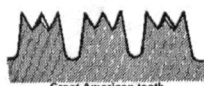
Great American tooth

Perforated lance tooth

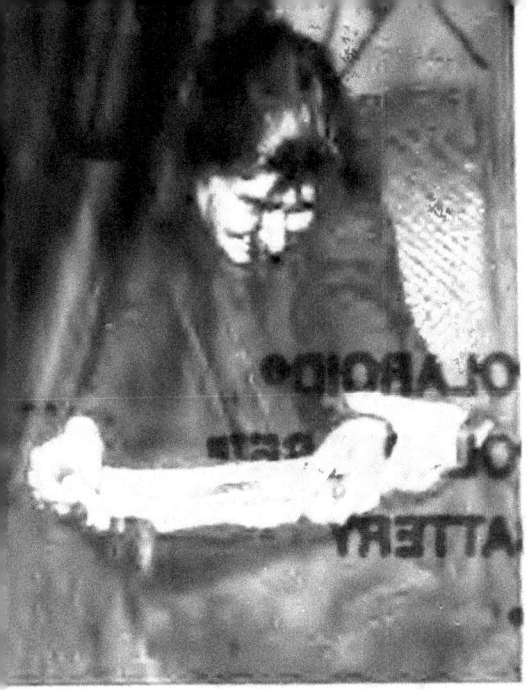

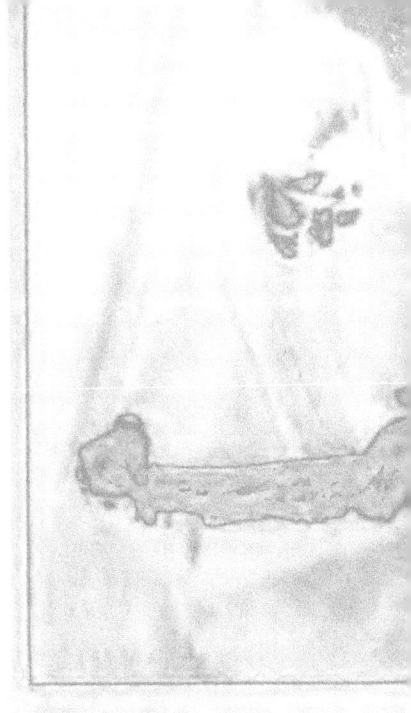

FIG. 201. TELEPLASM EMERGING FROM
THE HANDS.

FIG. 201. TELEPLASM EMER
THE HANDS.

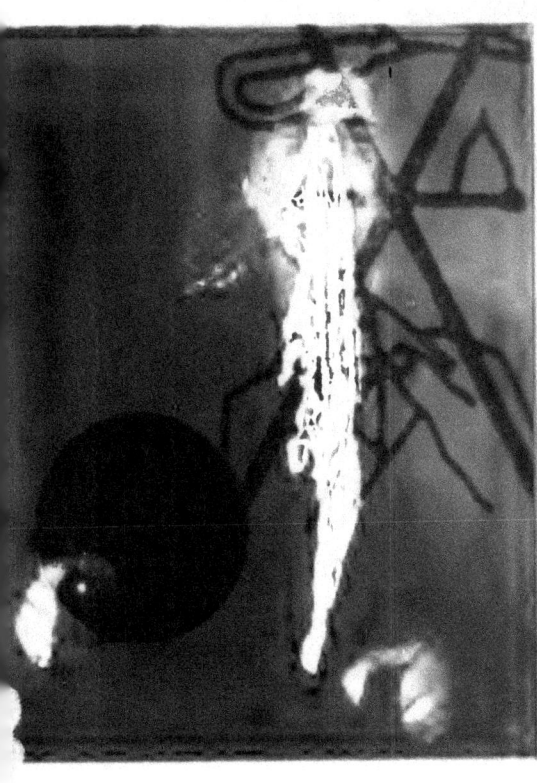

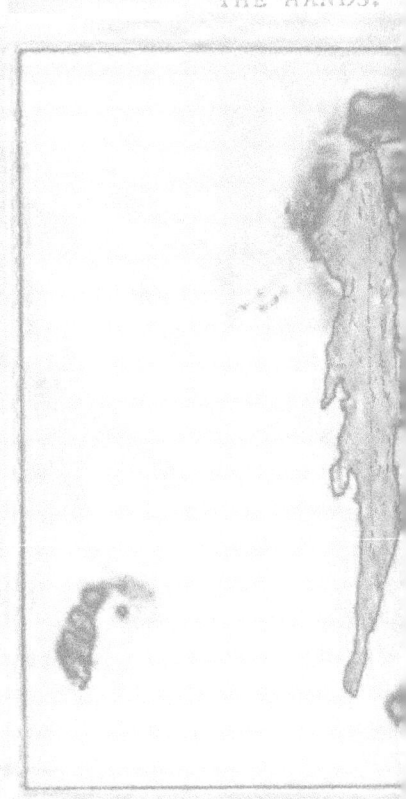

FIG. 202. EMERGENCE OF THE SUB-

FIG. 202. EMERGENCE OF

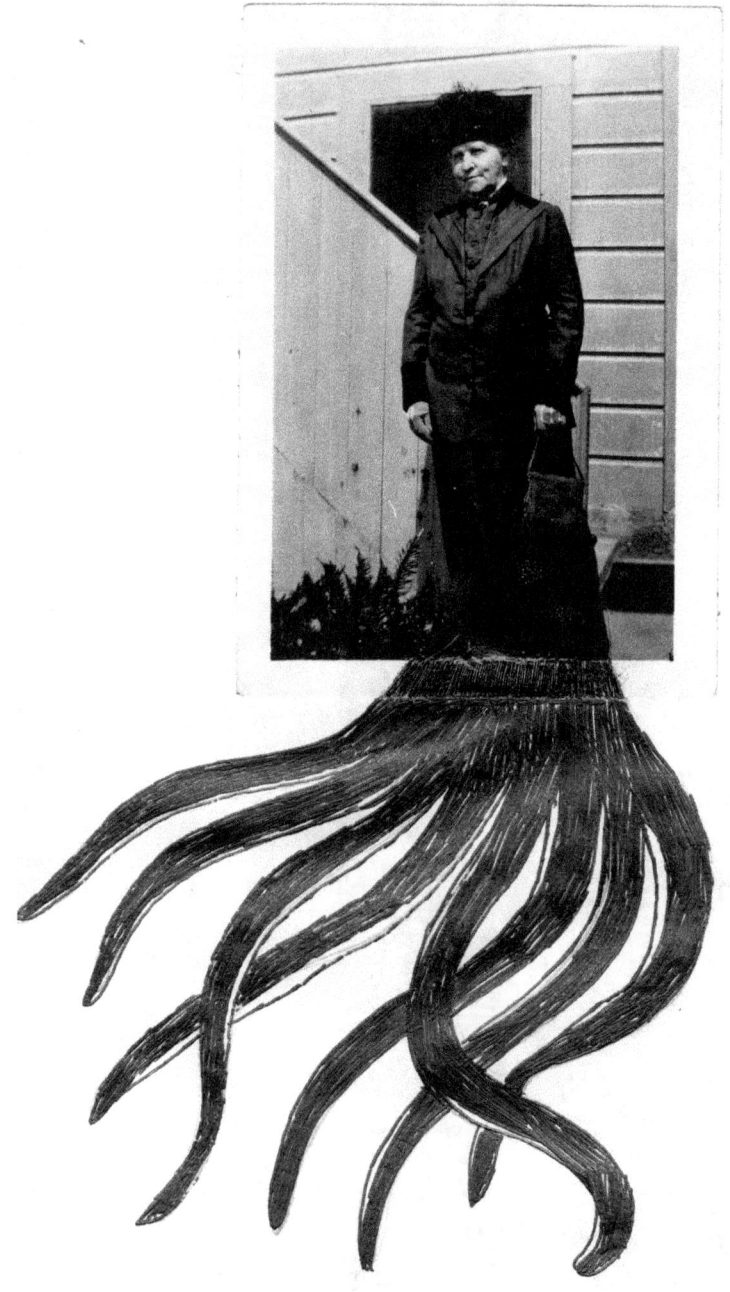

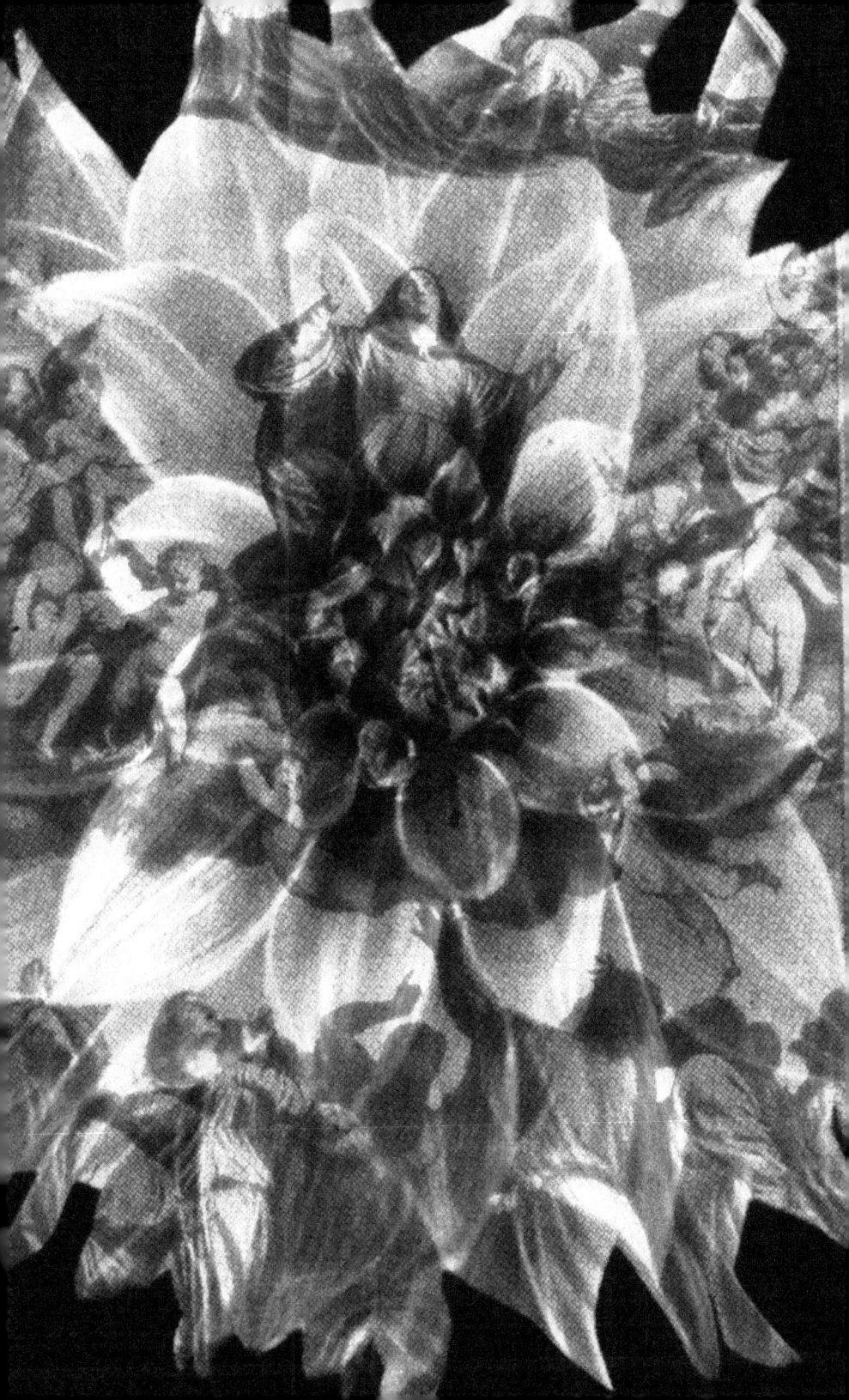

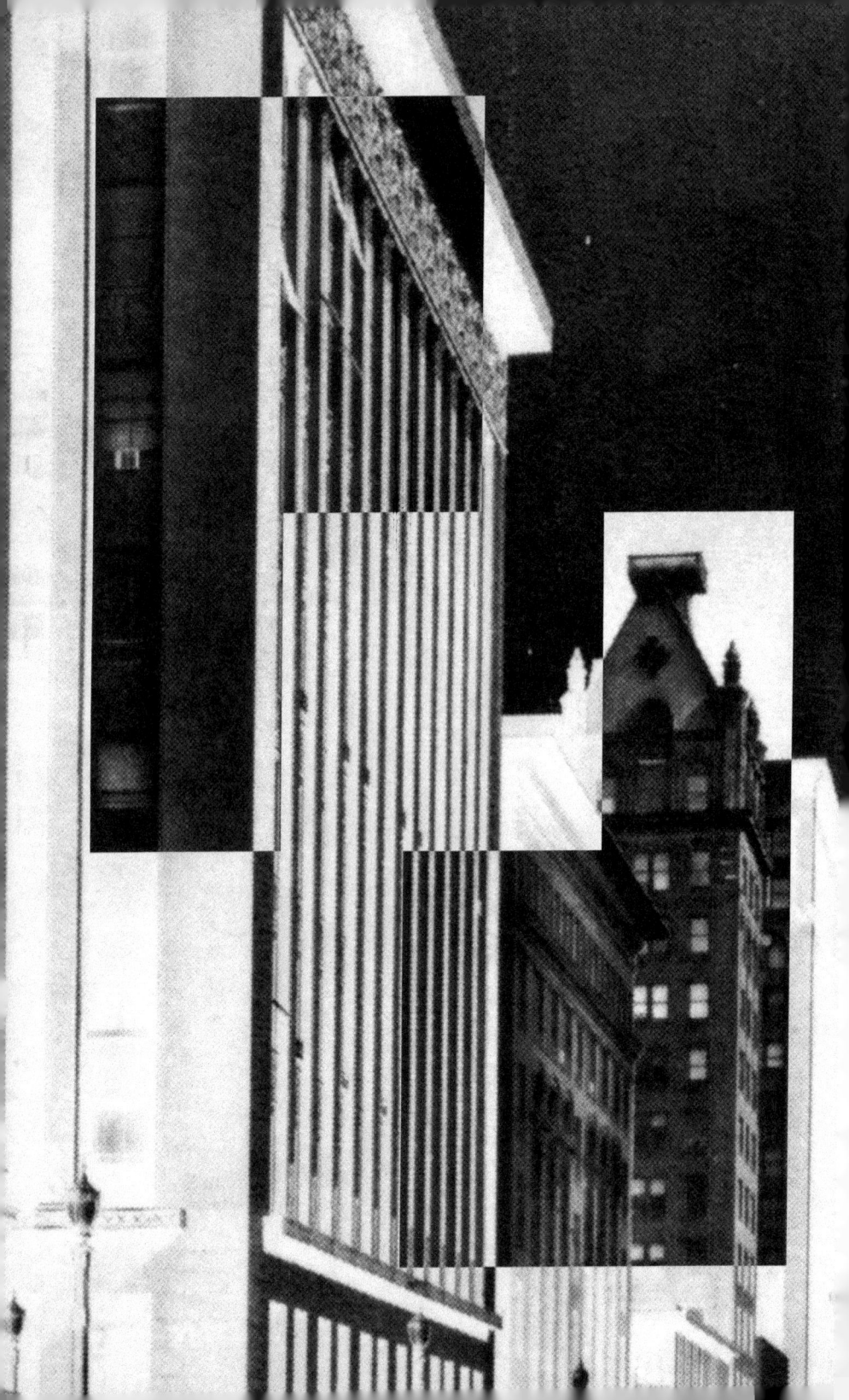

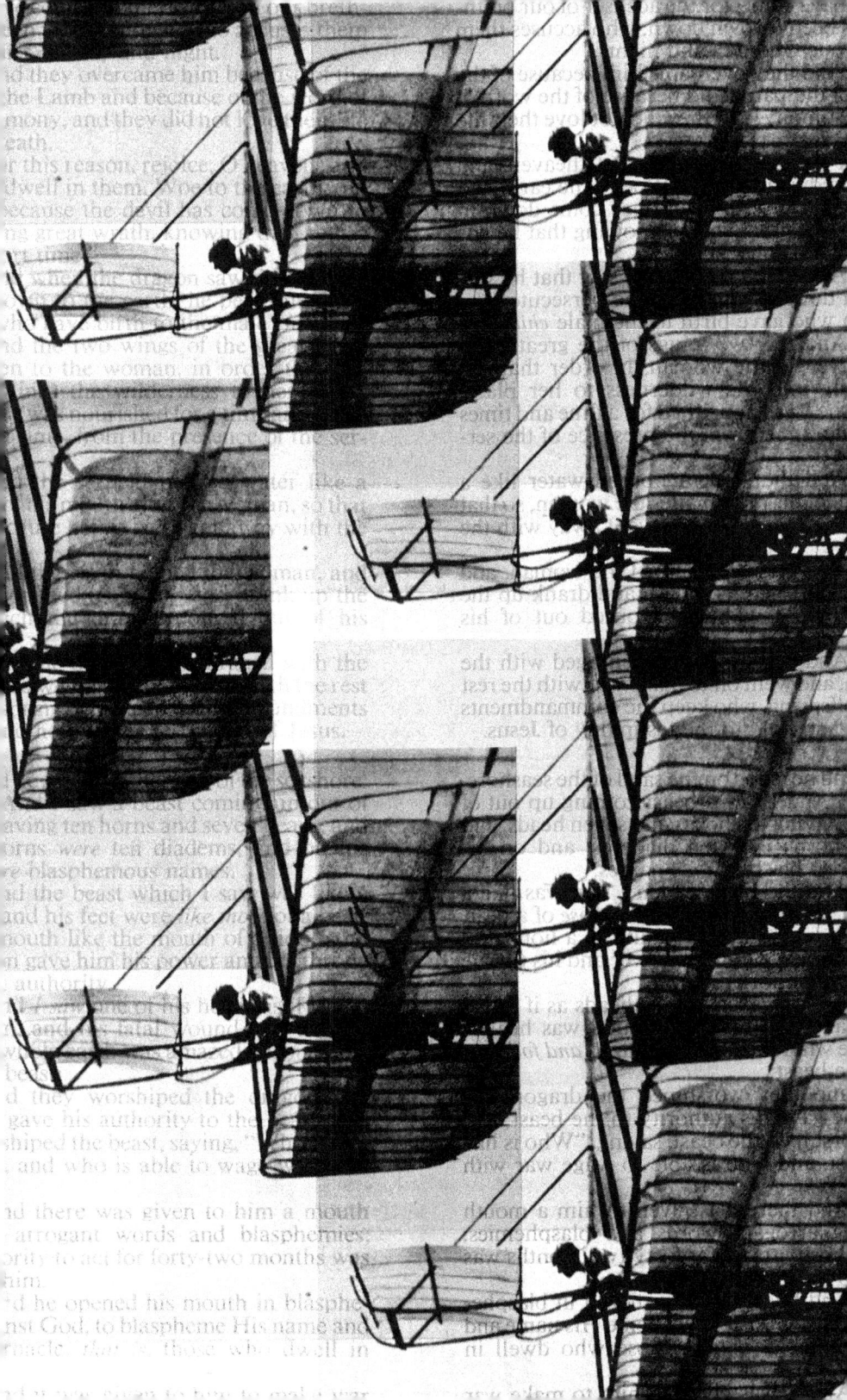

d they worshiped the
gave his authority to the
and who is able to wag
d there was given to him a mouth
arrogant words and blasphemies;
nst God, to blaspheme His name and

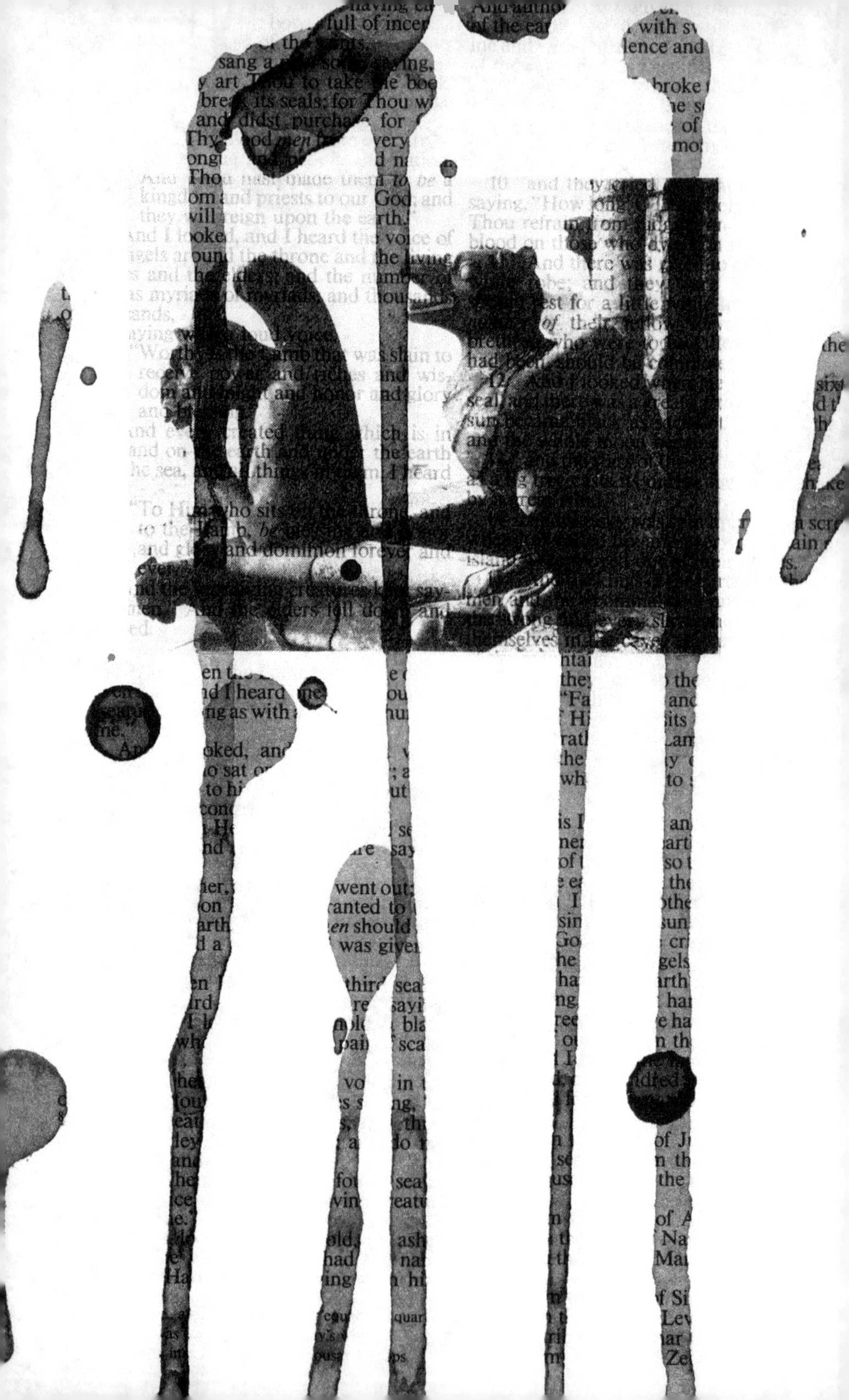

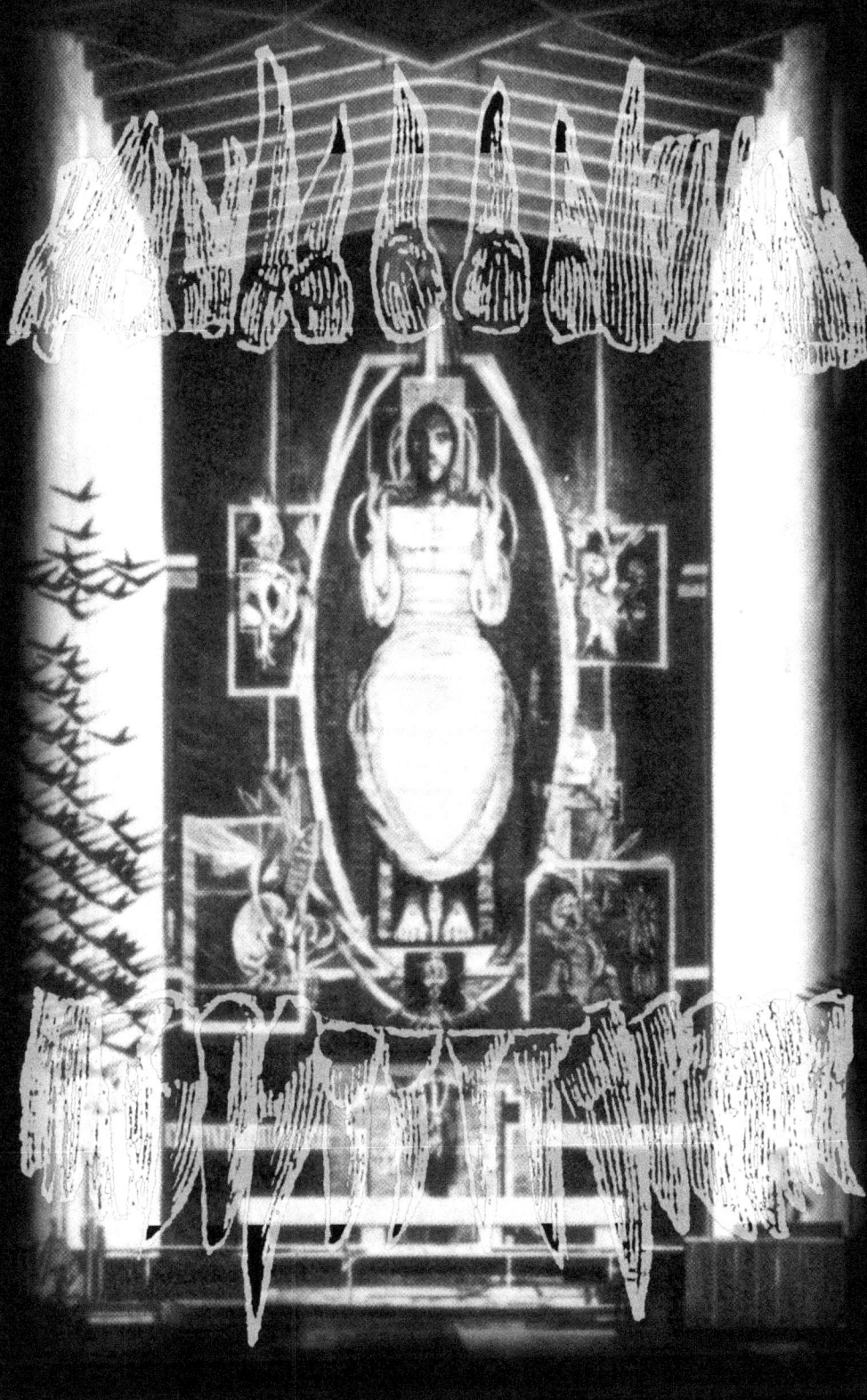

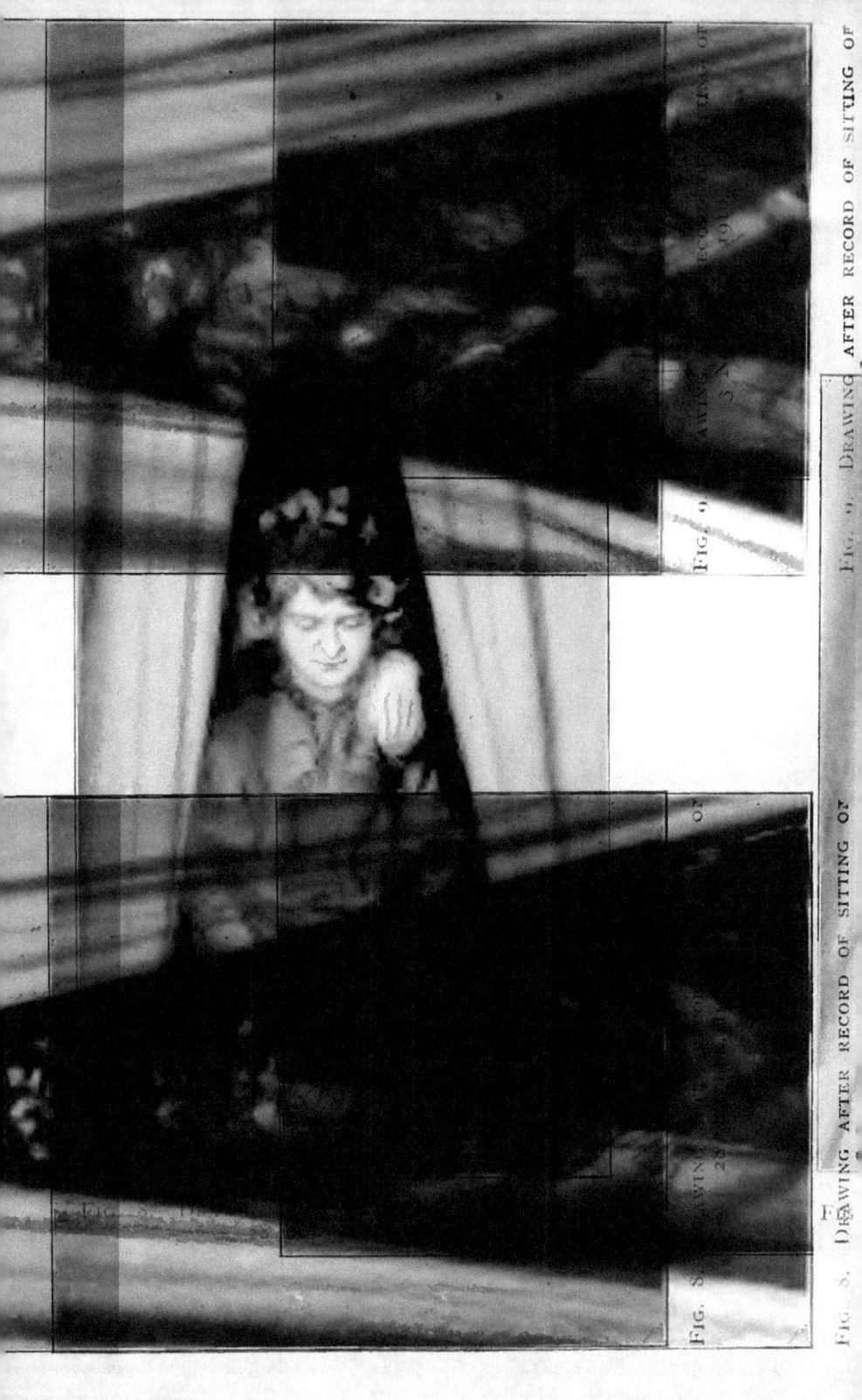

FIG. 8. DRAWING AFTER RECORD OF SITTING OF   FIG. 8. DRAWING AFTER RECORD OF SITTING OF

heir heads and
mourning, say
which had wh
er h, f
as
ven yo
be G
yo ain

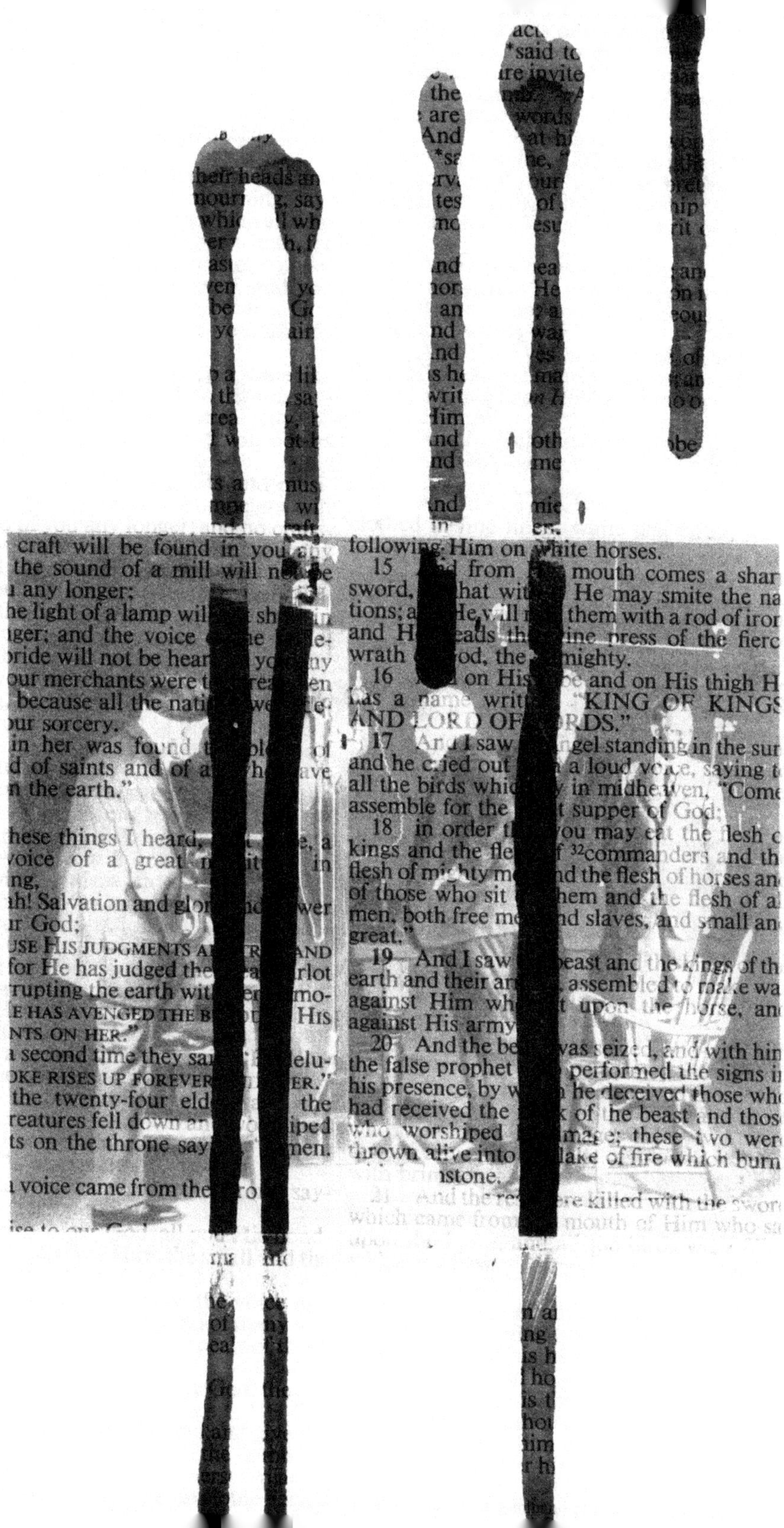

craft will be found in you any
the sound of a mill will not be
any longer;
he light of a lamp will not sh
ger; and the voice of the le-
bride will not be hear you any
our merchants were the great men
because all the natio were de-
our sorcery.
in her was found the blo of
d of saints and of a who ave
n the earth."

hese things I heard, a
voice of a great mult in
ng,
ah! Salvation and glor nd ower
r God;

USE HIS JUDGMENTS AR RU AND
for He has judged the rea rlot
rupting the earth with er mo-
E HAS AVENGED THE B OD His
NTS ON HER."

a second time they sa elu-
KE RISES UP FOREVER ER."
the twenty-four elde the
reatures fell down an iped
ts on the throne say men.

a voice came from the ro say

following Him on white horses.
15 nd from His mouth comes a shar
sword, hat wit He may smite the na
tions; a He will m them with a rod of iron
and H eads th ine press of the fierc
wrath od, the mighty.
16 on His e and on His thigh H
has a name writ "KING OF KINGS
AND LORD OF ORDS."
17 An I saw gel standing in the sun
and he c ied out a loud voice, saying t
all the birds which y in midheaven, "Come
assemble for the t supper of God;
18 in order t ou may eat the flesh
kings and the fle f commanders and th
flesh of mighty m nd the flesh of horses an
of those who sit hem and the flesh of a
men, both free me nd slaves, and small an
great."
19 And I saw beast and the kings of th
earth and their ar assembled to make wa
against Him wh t upon the horse, an
against His army
20 And the be as seiz d, and with him
the false prophet performed the signs i
his presence, by w h he deceived those who
had received the k of he beast and those
who worshiped image; these two wer
hrown alive into lake of fire which burn
nstone.
And the re re killed with the swor
which came fro mouth of Him who sa

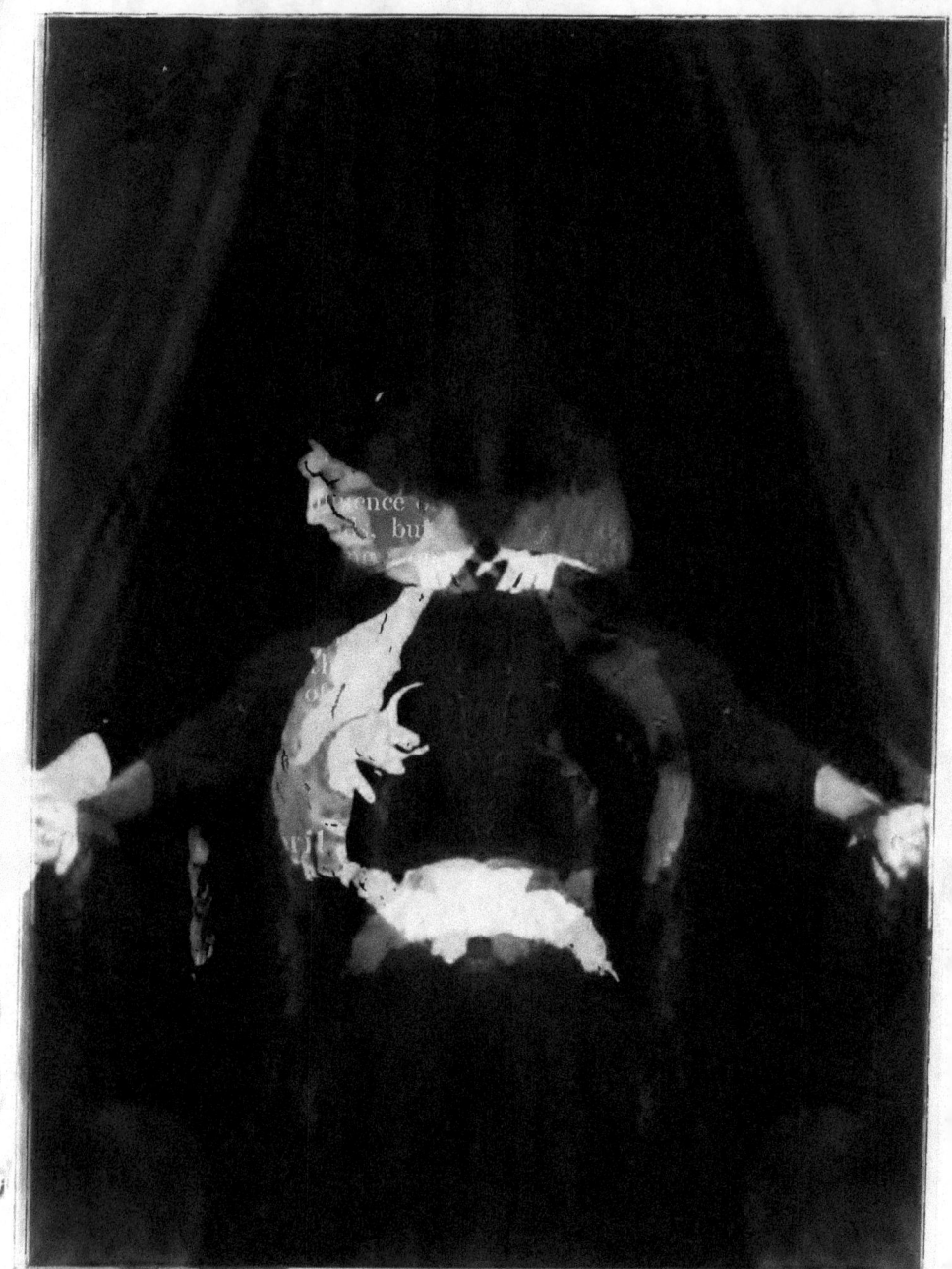

FIG. 27. FLASHLIGHT PHOTOGRAPH BY THE AUTHOR. 13 MARCH, 1911.

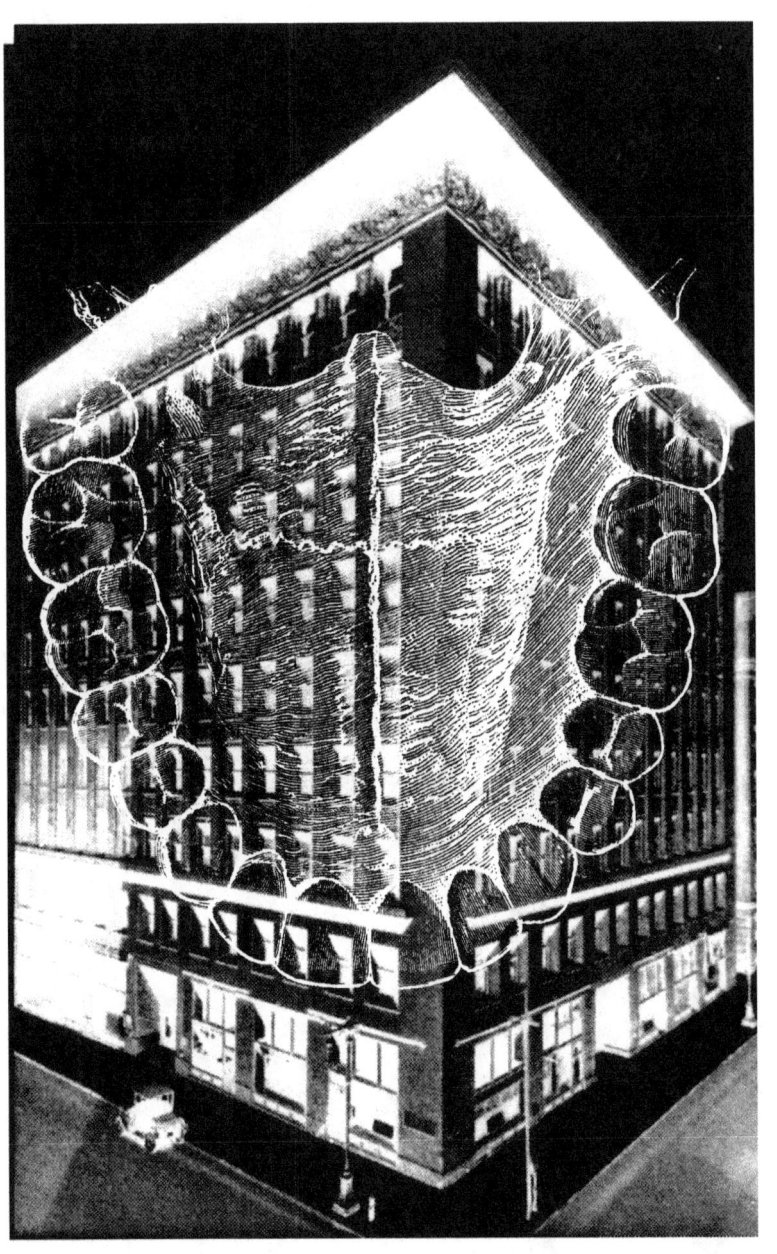

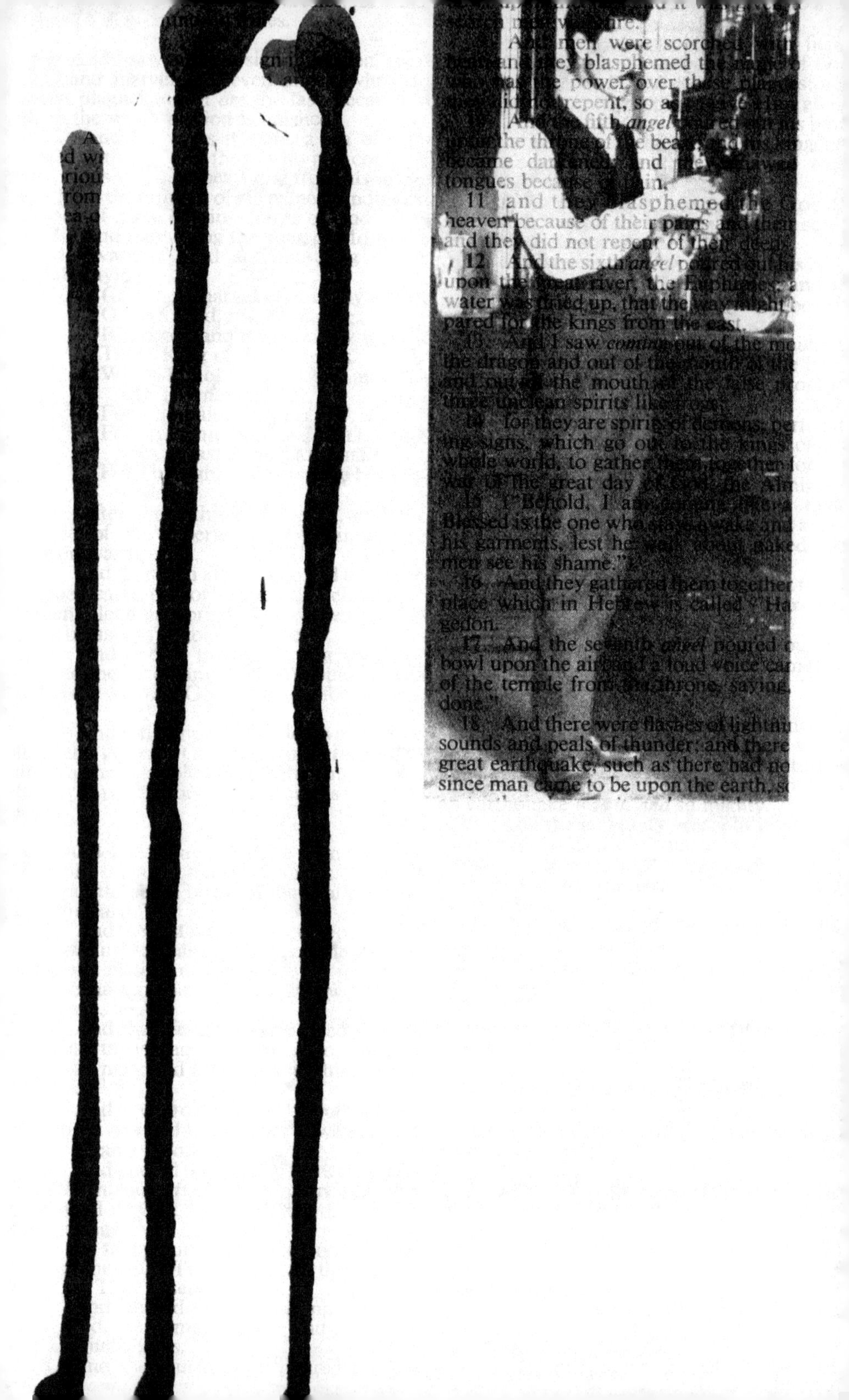

many shore.

And men were scorched with
heat, and they blasphemed the name of
... had the power over these plagues,
... did not repent, so as to ...

And the fifth *angel* poured out his
... the throne of the beast, and his ...
became darkened, and they ...
tongues because of pain.

11 and they blasphemed the ...
heaven because of their pains and their
and they did not repent of their deeds.

12 And the sixth *angel* poured out his
upon the great river, the Euphrates, and
water was dried up, that the way ...
pared for the kings from the east.

13 And I saw *coming out* of the m...
the dragon and out of the mouth of the ...
and out of the mouth of the false ...
three unclean spirits like frogs.

14 for they are spirits of demons, per...
ing signs, which go out to the kings ...
whole world, to gather them together ...
war of the great day of God the ...

15 ("Behold, I am coming like ...
Blessed is the one who stays awake and ...
his garments, lest he walk about naked ...
men see his shame.")

16 And they gathered them together ...
place which in Hebrew is called "Har...
gedon.

17 And the seventh *angel* poured ...
bowl upon the air, and a loud voice ca...
of the temple from the throne, saying ...
done."

18 And there were flashes of lightnin...
sounds and peals of thunder; and there ...
great earthquake, such as there had no...
since man came to be upon the earth, s...

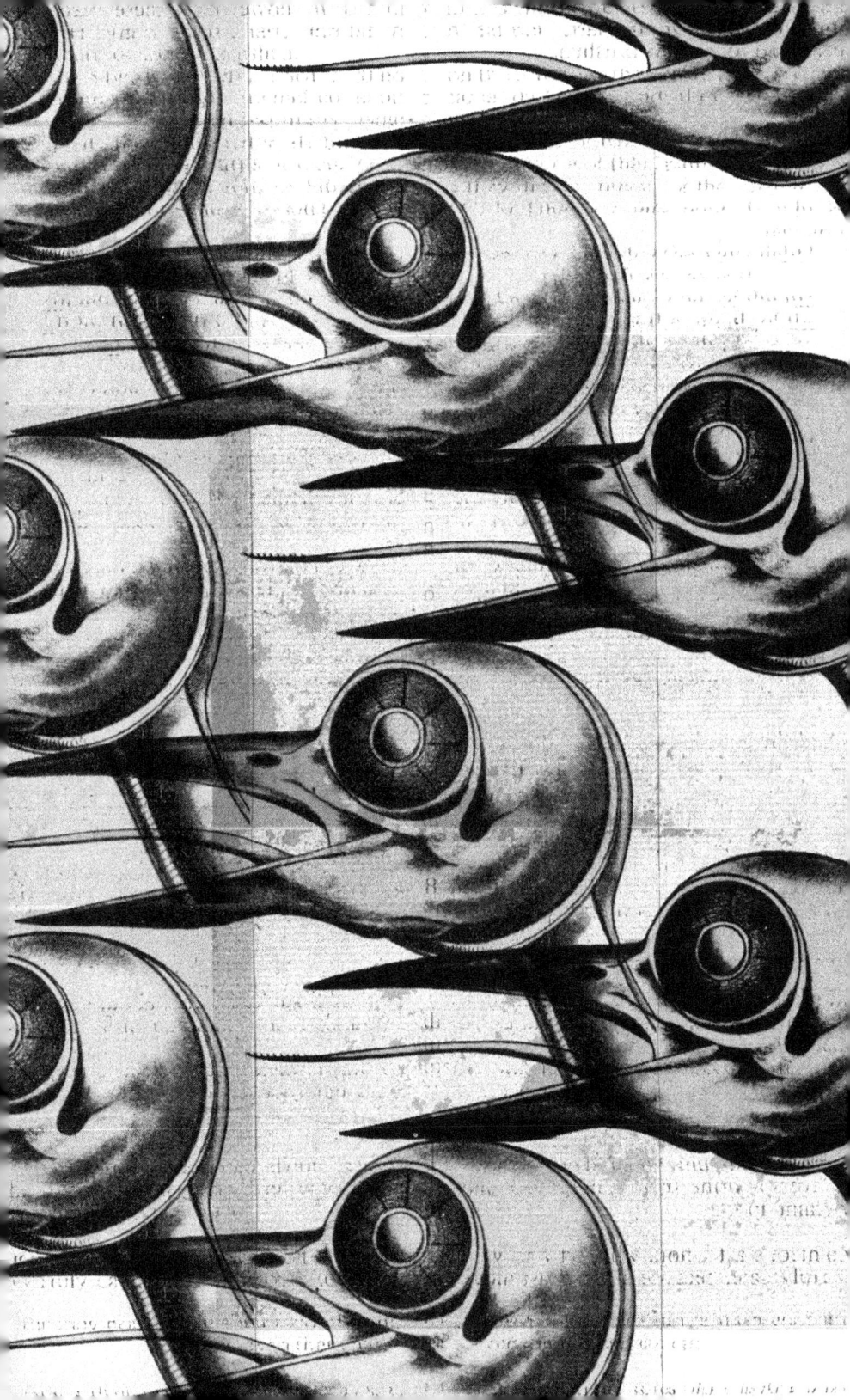

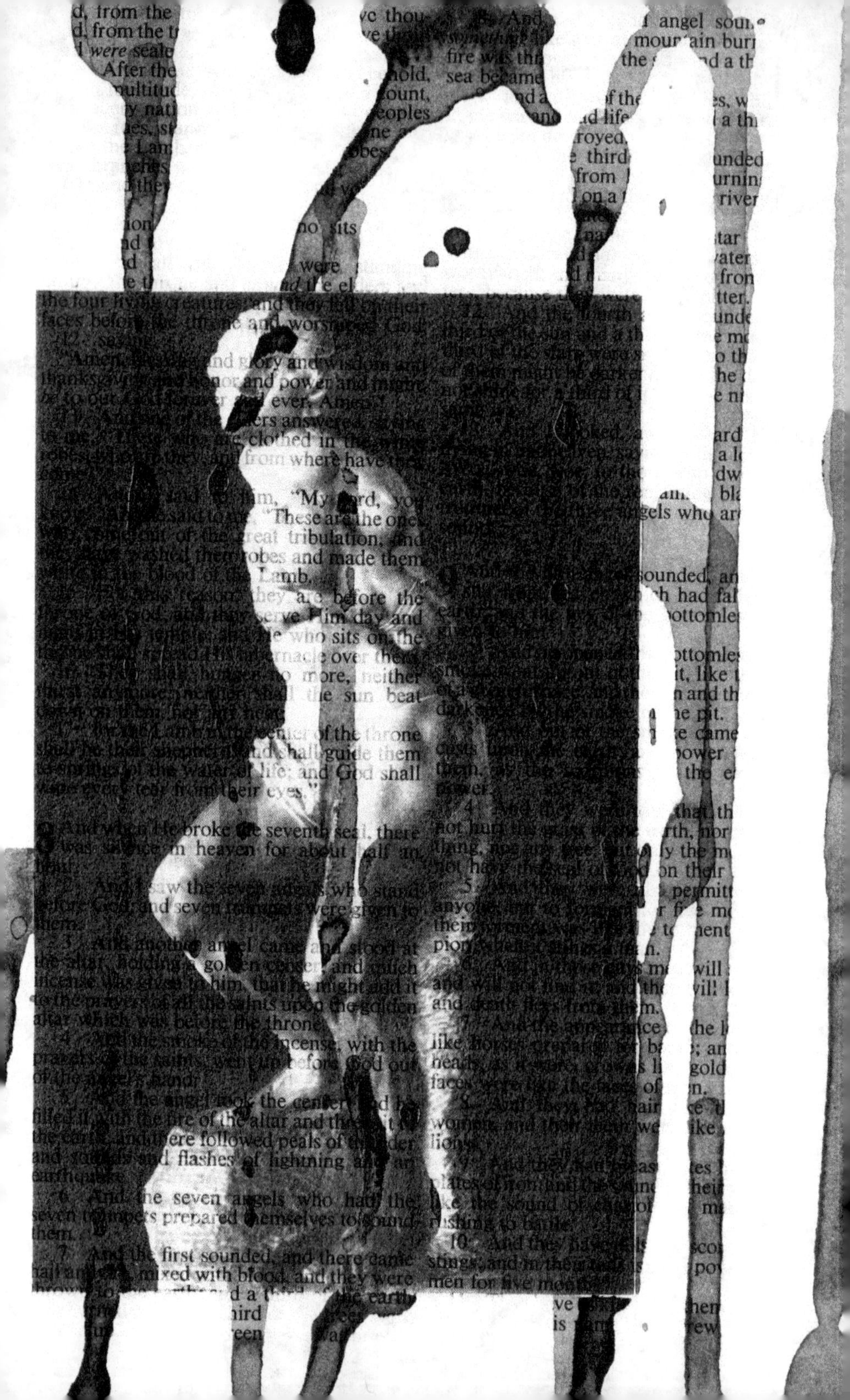

d, from the ... ve thou... ...s And ... l angel soun...
d, from the t... ve th... ...woman... ... moun ain burn
d *were* seal... fire was thr... the s... nd a th...
After the... old, sea became...
...ultitu... ...ount, ...nd ... of the ...es, w...
...y nati... ...eoples ...an... d life ... l a th...
...es, is... ...ne ...royed.
...Lam... ...obes ...e third ...unded
...ther ... of vo... from ... urning
...ion ... ...no sits ...on a ... river
...nd ... ...tar
...d ... were ... ...ater
...e t... ...and the el... ... fro...
the four living creatures and they fell ... their ... ...tter.
faces before the throne and worshiped God ... ...und...
...the ... sun ... a th... e m...
...Amen. ... and glory and wisdom and ... ...e dark... o th...
thanksgiving ... nor and power and might ... ...ird b... e ...
...to our ... r ever. Amen. ...e ni...
...ers answere... ...ard
...clothed in the ... ...a l...
...robes ... and from where have t... ...dw...
...am... bla...
...him, "My ...rd, yo... ...ngels who ar...
...said ... "These are the one...
...out of the great tribulation, and
...shed their robes and made them ...ounded, an...
...the blood of the Lamb. ...h had fal...
...before they are before the ... ...ottomles
...one of God, and they serve Him day and ...
...the ... ...le who sits on the ...ottomles
...and ... tabernacle over them. ...it, like t...
...hunger no more, neither ...n and th...
...nor ... ...ther shall the sun beat ...e pit.
...er of the throne ...e came
...shall ... ...shall guide them ...ower
...the water of life; and God shall ... the e...
...wipe every tear from their eyes." ...wer

And when He broke the seventh seal, there ...that th...
...silence in heaven for about half an ...not hurt the ... ...rth, nor
...ffing, nor any gree... ...ly the m...
...And I saw the seven angels who stand ...not have the seal of God on their
...God, and seven trumpets were given to ...
...them. ...permitt...
...And another angel came and stood at anyo... ...r five m...
...the altar, holding a golden censer; and much ...to ment
...incense was given to him, that he might add it pion ... ...man. ...
...to the prayers of all the saints upon the golden ...ays me will...
...altar which was before the throne. and will ... and they will...
...And the smoke of the incense, with the and death ... from them.
...prayers of the saints, went up before God out ...And the appearance ... the
...of the angel's hand. like horses prepared for ba... ...; an
...the angel took the censer, and he heads as it were crowns li... gold
...filled it with the fire of the altar and threw it to faces were like the faces of m...
...the earth; and there followed peals of thunder women, and their ... we... like
...and voices and flashes of lightning and an lions.
...earthquake. ...And they had bre... ...tes
...And the seven angels who had the plates of iron; and the ... their
...seven trumpets prepared themselves to sound like the sound of ... ... ma...
...them. ...rushing to battle.
...And the first sounded, and there came ...And they had ...scor
...hail and fire mixed with blood, and they were stings, and in their ... pow...
...thrown down to the earth; and a third ... the earth men for five mon...
...ird ...ve ...them
...een ...is ...rew

antly, flattering people for the sake of *gaining* advantage.

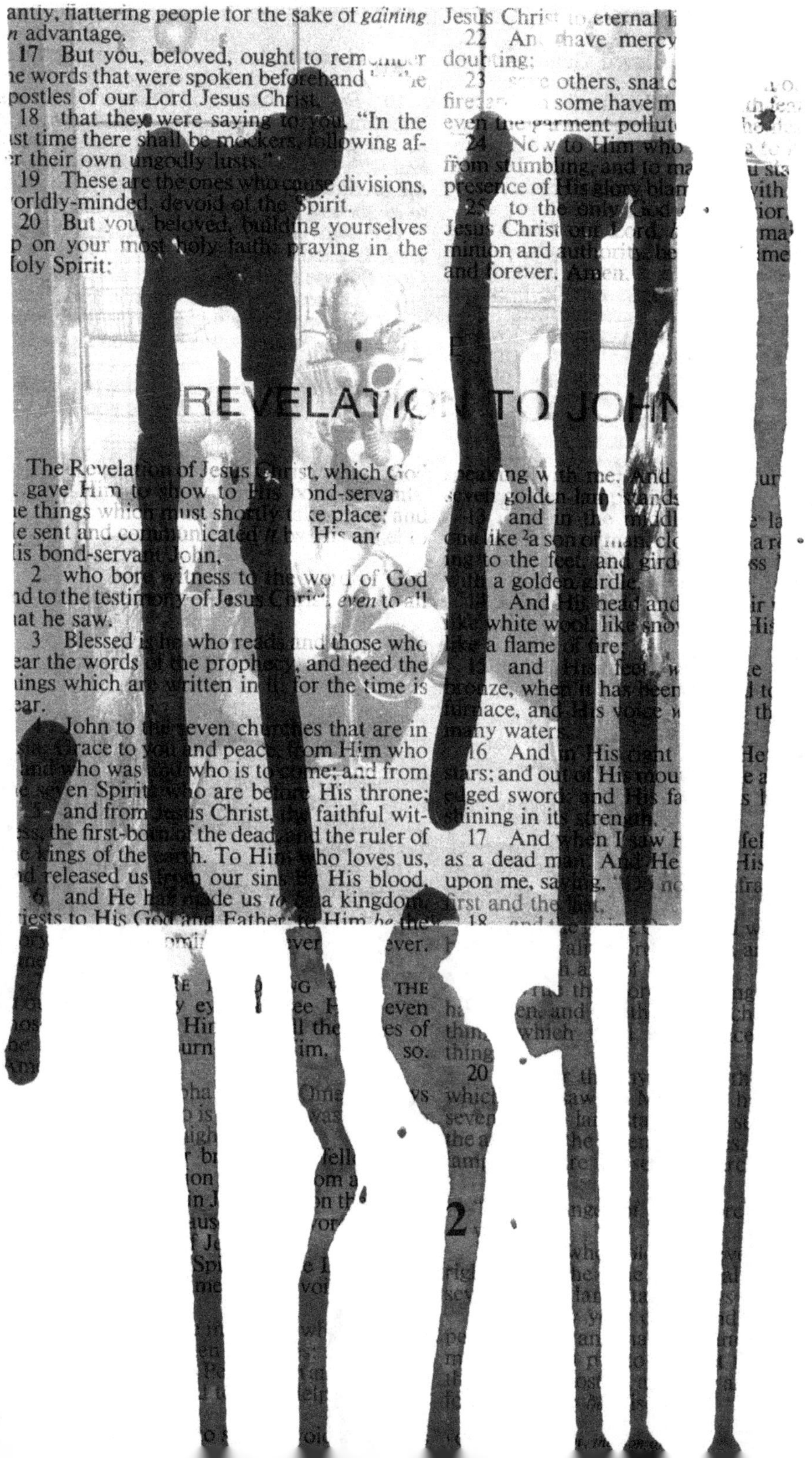

17 But you, beloved, ought to remember the words that were spoken beforehand by the apostles of our Lord Jesus Christ,

18 that they were saying to you, "In the last time there shall be mockers, following after their own ungodly lusts."

19 These are the ones who cause divisions, worldly-minded, devoid of the Spirit.

20 But you, beloved, building yourselves up on your most holy faith, praying in the Holy Spirit;

Jesus Christ to eternal life.

22 And have mercy doubting;

23 save others, snatc fire some have m even the garment pollute

24 Now to Him who from stumbling, and to ma presence of His glory blam

25 to the only God Jesus Christ our Lord, minion and authority, be and forever. Amen.

REVELATION TO JOHN

The Revelation of Jesus Christ, which God gave Him to show to His bond-servant the things which must shortly take place; and He sent and communicated it by His angel to His bond-servant John,

2 who bore witness to the word of God and to the testimony of Jesus Christ, even to all that he saw.

3 Blessed is he who reads and those who hear the words of the prophecy, and heed the things which are written in it; for the time is near.

John to the seven churches that are in Grace to you and peace, from Him who and who was and who is to come; and from the seven Spirits who are before His throne;

and from Jesus Christ, the faithful witness, the first-born of the dead and the ruler of the kings of the earth. To Him who loves us, and released us from our sins by His blood,

6 and He has made us to be a kingdom, priests to His God and Father; to Him be the

speaking with me. And seven golden lampstands;

and in the middle one like a son of man, clo ing to the feet, and gird with a golden girdle.

And His head and like white wool, like snow like a flame of fire;

and His feet w bronze, when it has been furnace, and His voice many waters.

16 And in His right stars; and out of His mou edged sword; and His fa shining in its strength.

17 And when I saw H as a dead man. And He upon me, saying, first and the la

18 and

20 which seven the a lam

2

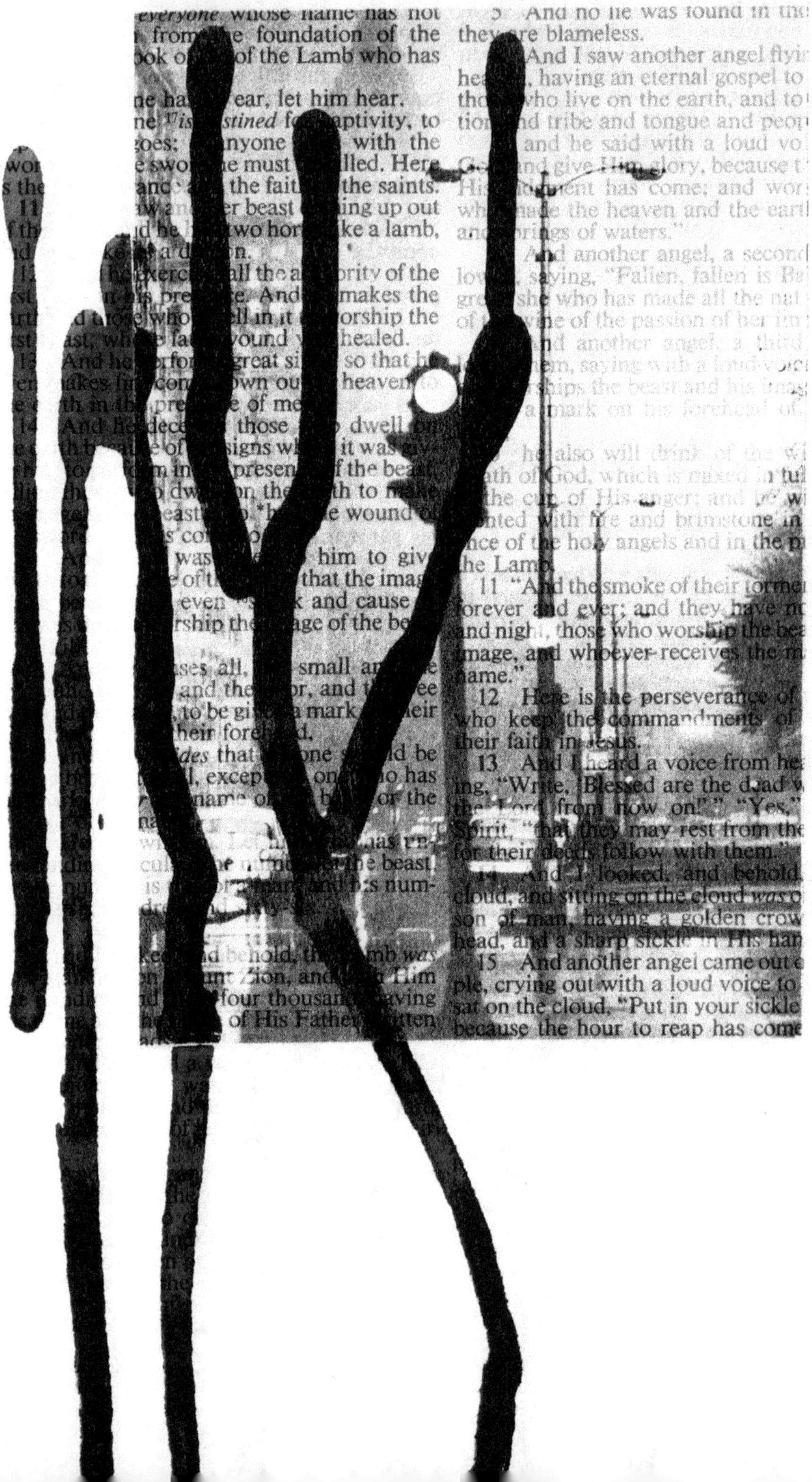

everyone whose name has not ... from ... foundation of the ... ook of ... of the Lamb who has ...

... has ... ear, let him hear. ... *is destined for* captivity, to ... goes; ... anyone ... with the ... sword ... must ... killed. Here ... and ... the faith ... the saints.

11 ... another beast ... ing up out ... he ... two horns ... ke a lamb, ...

... exercises all the authority of the ... presence. And ... makes the ... those who ... ell in it ... worship the ... ast; whose fatal wound ... healed. And he performs great signs ... so that he ... makes fire come down out of heaven ... th in the presence of men.

14 And he deceives those ... dwell on ... ... the ... of ... signs which it was ... ... in ... presence of the beast ... o dwell on the ... th to make ... east ... *the wound of* ... s ... was ... him to giv ... ... of t ... that the imag ... even ... k and cause ... ... ship the image of the be ...

... ses all, ... small and ... and the ... or, and the ... to be given a mark ... their forehead. ... that ... one ... ld be ... l, except ... one who has ... name o ... b ... or the ... na ... ... Let ... who has un ... cula ... e number of the beast, ... is ... the ... man; and his num ...

... d ... ... keep ... d behold, the ... mb *was* ... on ... unt Zion, and ... Him ... ... four thousand ... having ... s of His Father ... tten ...

5. And no lie was found in the ... they are blameless.

... And I saw another angel flyin ... hea ... having an eternal gospel to ... tho ... who live on the earth, and to ... tion ... d tribe and tongue and peop ... ... and he said with a loud vo ... G ... and give Him glory, because t ... His ... ... ment has come; and wor ... wh ... ... de the heaven and the earth ... and ... rings of waters."

... And another angel, a second ... lo ... saying, "Fallen, fallen is Ba ... gre ... she who has made all the nat ... of ... ine of the passion of her im ... ... d another angel, a third ... em, saying with a loud voic ... ... ships the beast and his imag ... ... a mark on his forehead, of ...

... he also will drink of the wi ... th of God, which is mixed in ful ... the cup of His anger; and he wi ... ... nted with fire and brimstone in ... ... nce of the holy angels and in the p ... the Lamb.

11 "And the smoke of their tormen ... forever and ever; and they have no ... and night, those who worship the bea ... image, and whoever receives the m ... name."

12 Here is the perseverance of ... who keep the commandments of ... their faith in Jesus.

13 And I heard a voice from hea ... ing, "Write, Blessed are the dead w ... the Lord from now on!'" "Yes," ... Spirit, "that they may rest from the ... for their deeds follow with them."

... And I looked, and behold ... cloud, and sitting on the cloud *was* ... son of man, having a golden crow ... head, and a sharp sickle in His han ...

15 And another angel came out o ... ple, crying out with a loud voice to ... sat on the cloud, "Put in your sickle ... because the hour to reap has come

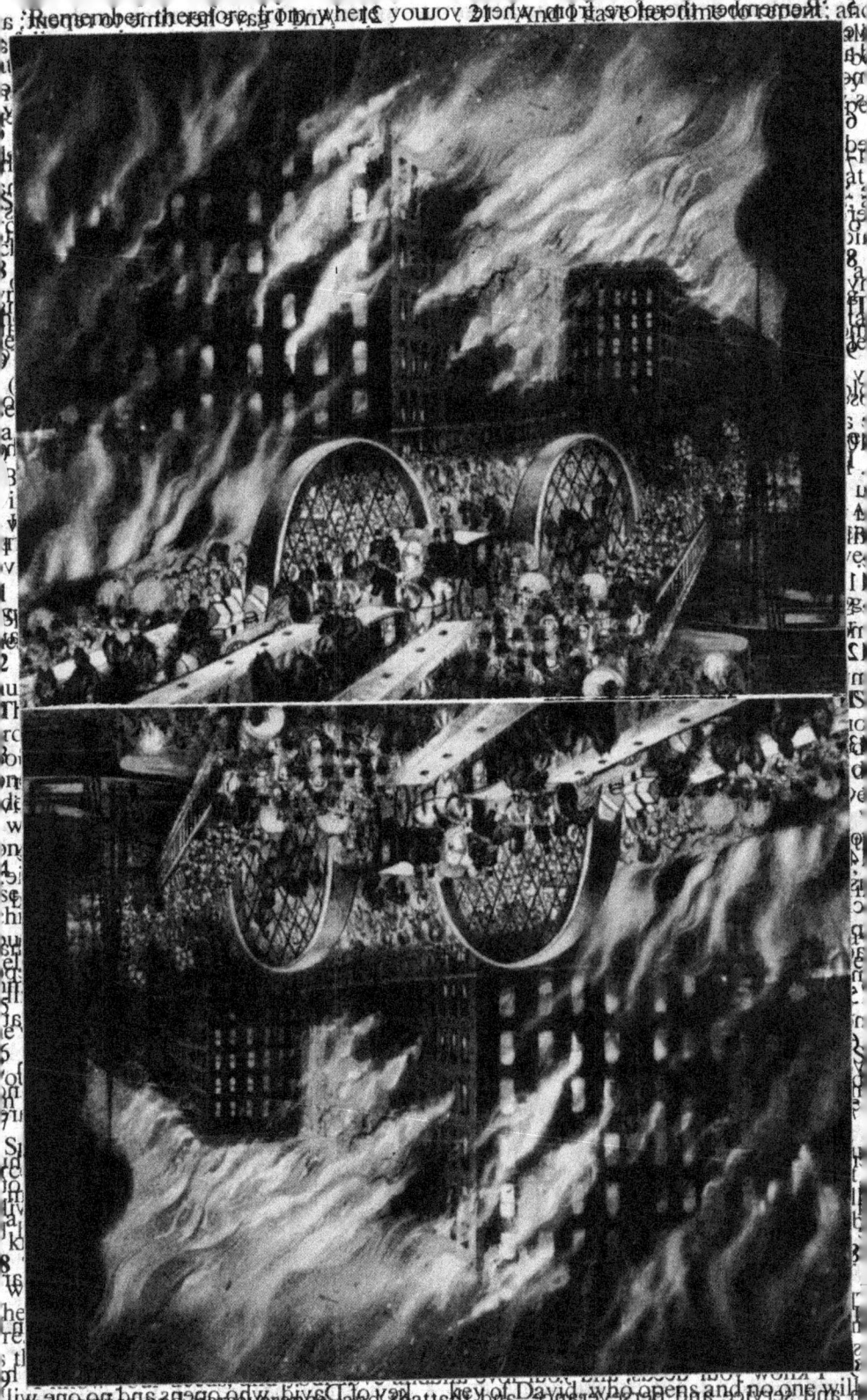

ny. This step eliminated the
-of her mediumistic power, f
e from various quarters. It
control of the young girl
thy and uninterrupted observa
and more.

Sittings of October and

PREPA

During the last series of sitti
ged beside a window, which
was occasionally inconvenienc
ged the cabinet on the opposi
enlarged it. All the walls,
ing, sewn together by ma
showed not the slightest op
I may here mention s
 utely examined by me, before a
an electric lamp. There was
one could put a finger. E
touched the cabinet ther
of the cabinet was l
depth 4 feet. Above, it
by a roof so that it w

er of the professional ex...

which favourable proposals had...
only enabled her to exercise...
ode of life, but also to...
of her powers, which developed...
come from various quarters. It no...
absolute control of the young girl's
lengthy and uninterrupted observati...
more and more.

ovember 1910 (Paris).

ONS.

Sittings of ...ctober and

in Paris, the d...k cabinet was
not close perfe...y. Since Eva
by the draugh... Mme. Bisson
de of the room ...d at the same
floor and the ... consisted...
e, in such a way that the...
g, and appeared to be made...
ally that the cabinet was most...
after every sitting, with the help...
the slightest opening through...
where the narrow side of the...
as a wall of the black material,
r than before. Length 7 feet
entirely closed off at a height
have been impossible to intro-

re still [...] ng after the [...] ings.

13 A [...] e sixth a [...] sounded, and I heard a [...] e from the [...] ur horns of the golden a [...] which is bef [...] God,

14 on [...] ying to the [...] h angel who had the trump [...] "Release the [...] ur angels who are bound at [...] great river [...] rates."

15 An [...] ne four ange [...] ho had been prepared for [...] e hour and [...] and month and year, wer [...] eleased, so t [...] hey might kill a third of m [...] kind.

16 An [...] ne number [...] the armies of the horsemen [...] s two hun [...] d million; I heard he numb [...] f them.

17 An [...] is is how [...] w in the vision the orses an [...] ose who s [...] n them: the riders ad brea [...] tes the co [...] of fire and of hyainth and [...] brimstone [...] d the heads of the orses ar [...] e the hea [...] f lions; and out of heir mo [...] proceed [...] e and smoke and rimston [...]

18 A [...] d of manki [...] was killed by these hree pla [...] , by the fi [...] nd the smoke and he brim [...] e, which [...] eeded out of their mouths.

19 Fo [...] e power of [...] horses is in their mouths a [...] h their tails [...] their tails are like erpents [...] have head [...] d with them they o harm [...]

20 A [...] he rest of m [...] nd, who were not illed by [...] se plagues, [...] not repent of the works of [...] r hands, so [...] ot to worship demons, an [...] e idols of go [...] nd of silver and of rass and [...] stone and of [...] od, which can neither see nor hear nor w [...]

21 and they did no [...] ent of their murders nor of their sorceri [...] or of their immoality nor of their thefts.

10 And I saw another strong angel coming down out of heaven, clothed with a loud; and the rainbow was upon his head, nd his face was like the sun, and his feet like illars of fire;

2 and he had in his hand a little book which was open. And he placed his right foot n the sea and his left on the land;

3 and he cried out with a loud voi [...]

8 And the voice [...] heaven, I heard again [...] saying, "Go, take the [...] the hand of the angel [...] and on the land."

9 And I went to t [...] give me the little boo [...] "Take it, and eat it; [...] stomach bitter, but in [...] sweet as honey."

10 And I took the [...] angel's hand and ate it, [...] sweet as honey; and w [...] stomach was made bit [...]

11 And they *sai [...] prophesy again concer [...] nations and tongues a [...]

11 And [...] re was gi [...] like [...] ff; and s [...] measure [...] mple of [...] those wh [...] orship in [...]

2 "An [...] eave out [...] side the te [...] ple, and c [...] has been [...] en to the [...] tread un [...] foot the [...] months.

3 "An [...] I will gra [...] witnesses [...] nd they w [...] hundred [...] sixty day [...]

4 Th [...] are the [...] two lamp [...] ds that s [...] the earth [...]

5 A [...] f anyone [...] fire proce [...] out of th [...] their ene [...] s; and if a [...] harm the [...] n this ma [...]

6 Th [...] have the [...] sky, in o [...] that rain [...] days of [...] r prophe [...] power ov [...] e waters [...] and to s [...] the earth [...] often as t [...] desire.

7 A [...] hen they [...] timony, t [...] east tha [...] abyss will [...] e war w [...] them and [...] them

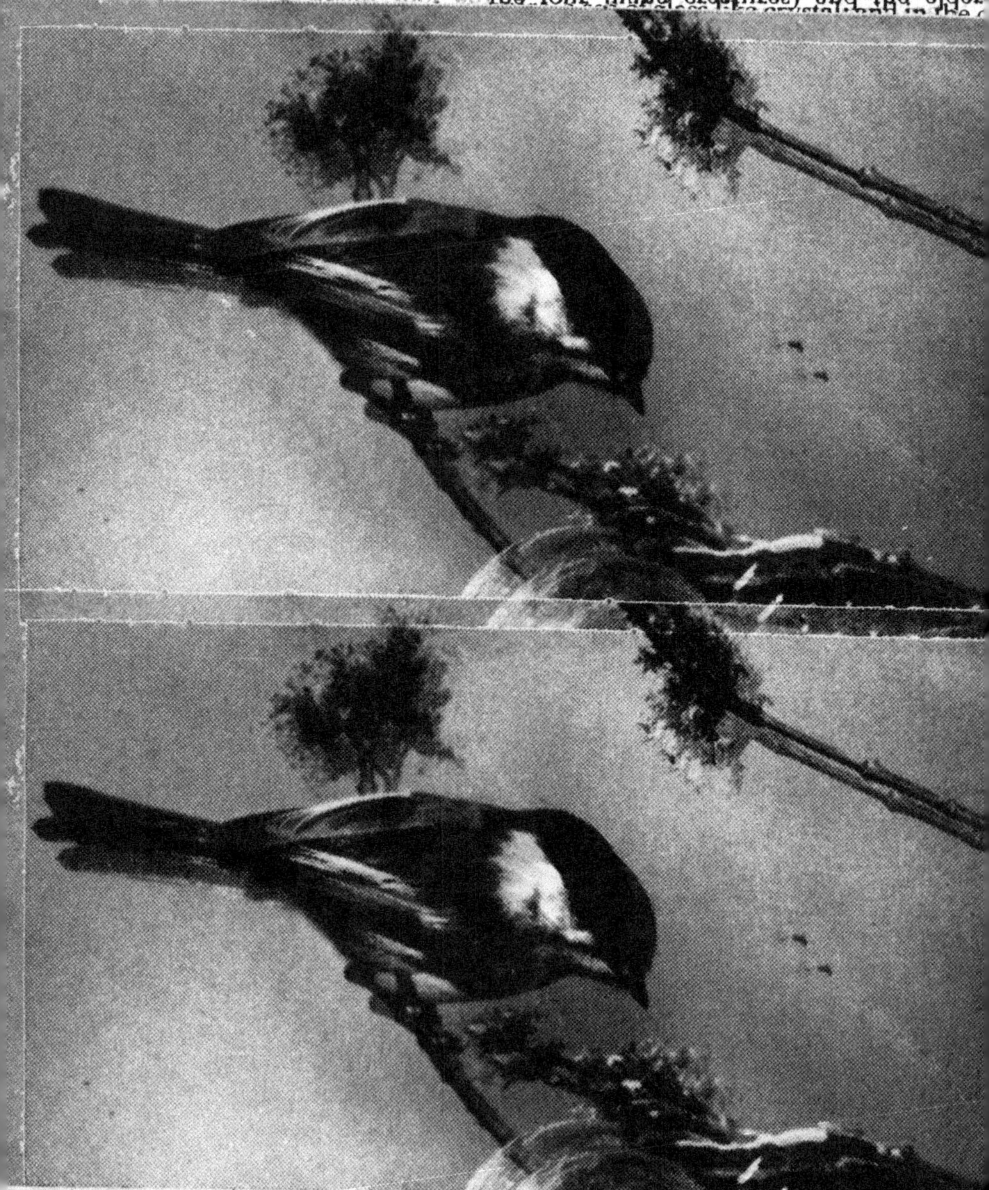

garments, and golden crowns on their he
5 And from the throne proceed flash
lightning and sounds and peals of thun
And *there were* seven lamps of fire burning
fore the throne, which are the seven Spirit
God.

ter these things I looked, and behold, a
oor *standing* open in heaven, and the first
which I had heard, like *the sound* of a
et speaking with me, said, "Come up
and I will show you what must take
after these things."
Immediately I was in the Spirit; and
d, a throne was standing in heaven, and

the four living creatures) and the elder
Lamb standing, as if slain, having seven ho
and seven eyes, which are the seven Spiri
God, sent out into all the earth.
7 And He came, and He took *it* out of
right hand of Him who sat on the throne
8 And when He had taken the book
four living creatures and the twenty-fou

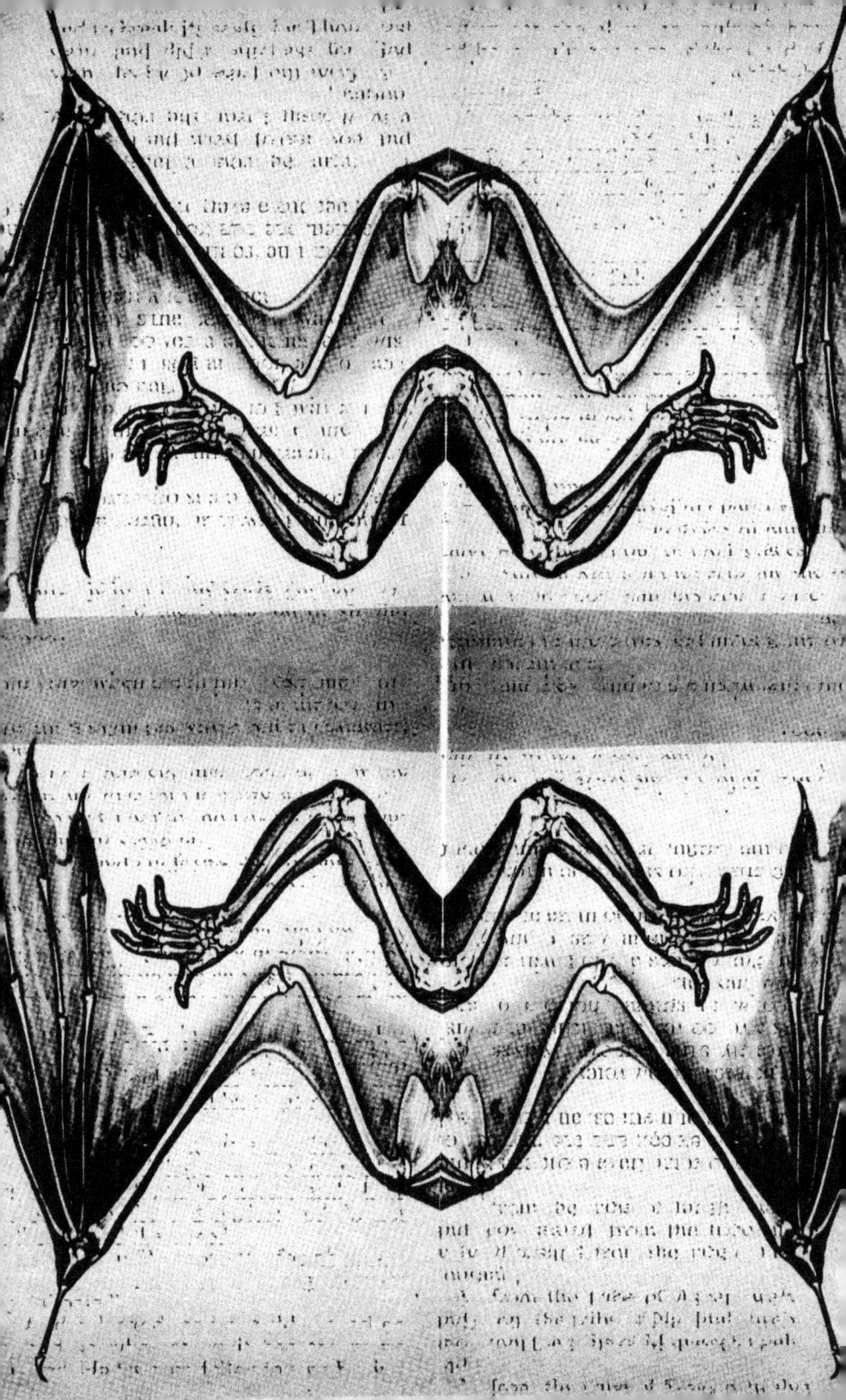

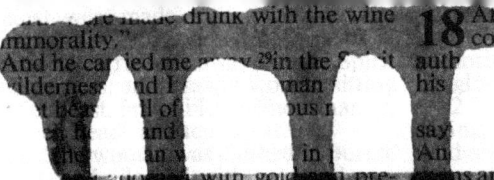

made drunk with the wine
immorality."
And he carried me ... 29in the ...
wilderness. And I ... man
... full of ...
... an ... in ...

... with gold, pre-
... having in ... and a
... abominations and ... the un-
... immorality
... her ... head a ... was
... BABYLON ... THE
MOTHER OF H ... LOTS
ABOMINATIONS ... THE

... the woman drunk ... the
... and ... the blood of the
... And ... en I saw h ... won-

... angel sa ... me, "Wh ... do you
... tell y ... the mystery ... of the
... beast ... carries h ... which
... ds and ... the ten hor ...
... that y ... saw was a ... not,
... come up ... of the a ... and
... tion. An ... hose who ... ll on
... onder ... ose name ... not
... book ... life from ... oun-
... ld, wh ... they see t ... beast,
... not a ... will come ...
... min ... hich has ... dom.
... s are ... en mount ... on
... oman sits ...
... hey are se ... kings; fi ... ha ...
... the other h ... not yet co ... an ...
... hes, he must ... main a litt ... hile.
... he beast whi ... was and is not, is
... an eighth, ar ... is one of the ... even,
... to destruction ...
... he ten horn ... hich you ... y are
... ho have not ... received ... ting-
... y receive au ... rity as kin ... with ...
... one hour.
... have one p ... ose and th ... giv ...
... and authori ... to the beas ...
... will wage w ... against the ... amb,
... b will ove ... ome them, b ... ause
... lords an ... King of king ... and
... e with Hi ... are the calle ... and
... aithful."
... e said to me ... The waters ... ich

... ns and a prison of every unclea ...
... rison of every unclean an ... hate
... "For all the nations ... have d ...
... e of the passion of her immoral ...
... ings of the earth have committed
... rality with her, and the merch ...
... h have become rich by the w ...
... uality."
... And I heard another ...
... ven, saying, "Come out of ...
... you may not partici ... n h ...
... you may not receive ... her pl ...
... for her sins have ... ed up ...
... ven, and God has remembered
... "Pay her back even ... s she ha ...
... back to her double according to ...
... he cup which she has mixed, m ...
... ch for her.
... "To the degree that she glori ...
... lived sensuously, to the same ...
... torment and mourning; for she ...
... rt, 'I SIT as A QUEEN and I ...
... ow, and will never see mourn ...
... "For this reason in one da ...
... come, pestilence and mournin ...
... and she will be burned up with ...
... d God who judges her is stron ...
... "And the kings of the earth ...
... ted acts of immorality and lived ...
... her, will weep and lament ove ...
... y see the smoke of her burning ...
... standing at a distance beca ...
... of her torment, saying, 'Woe ...
... eat city, Babylon, the strong city ...
... h ... your judgment has come.'
... "And the merchants of the ...
... mourn over her, because no ...
... t ... cargoes any more;
... cargoes of gold and silver an ...
... s ... es and pearls and fine linen a ...
... a ... ilk and scarlet, and every ki ...
... w ... and every article of ivory an ...
... t ... made from very costly wood ...
... a ... on and marble;

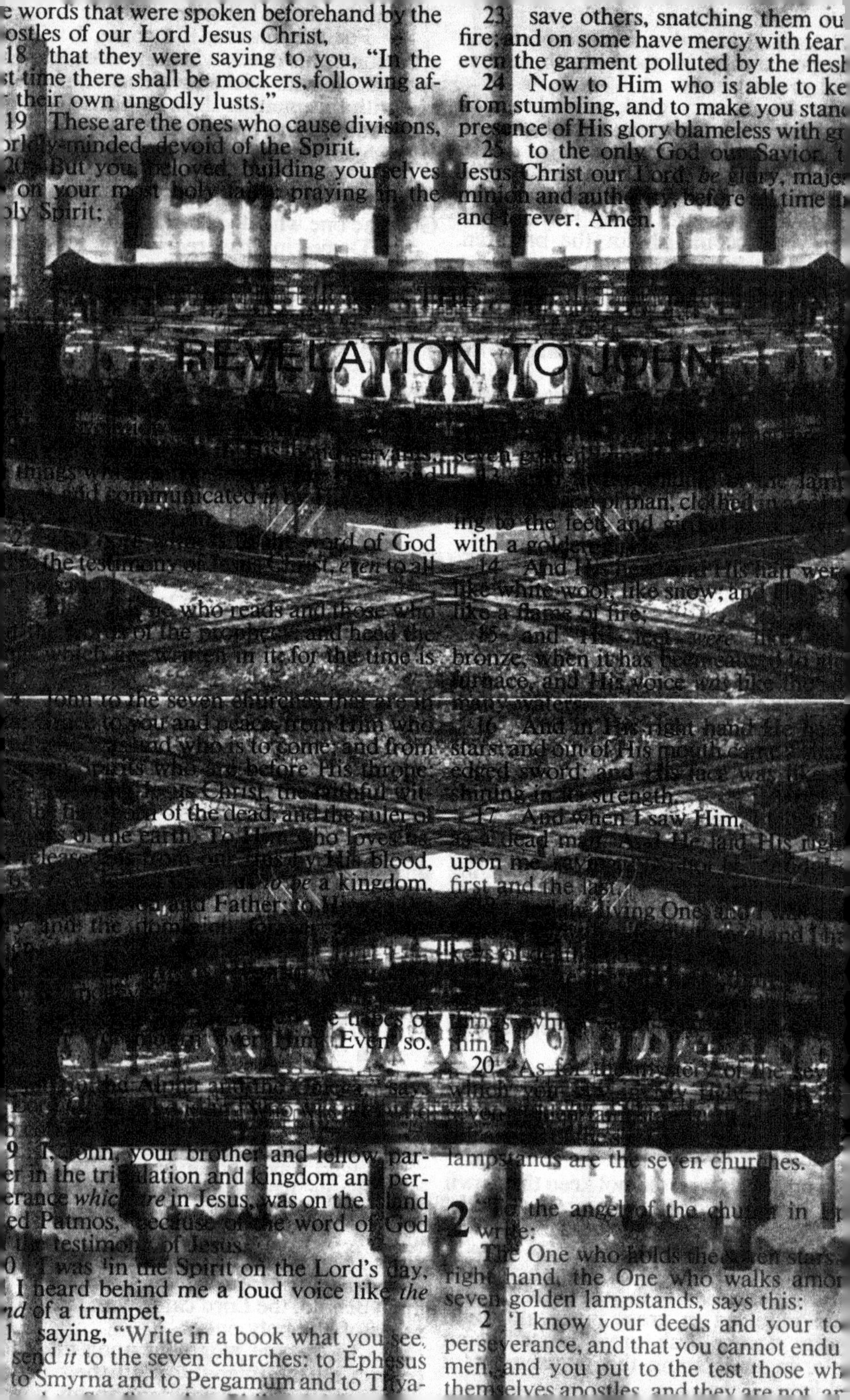

e words that were spoken beforehand by the
ostles of our Lord Jesus Christ,

18 that they were saying to you, "In the
st time there shall be mockers, following af-
their own ungodly lusts."

19 These are the ones who cause divisions,
orldly-minded, devoid of the Spirit.

20 But you, beloved, building yourselves
on your most holy faith, praying in the
oly Spirit;

23 save others, snatching them ou
fire; and on some have mercy with fear
even the garment polluted by the flesh

24 Now to Him who is able to ke
from stumbling, and to make you stand
presence of His glory blameless with gr

25 to the only God our Savior,
Jesus Christ our Lord, be glory, maje
minion and authority, before all time a
and forever. Amen.

REVELATION TO JOHN

word of God
the testimony of Jesus Christ, even to all

who reads and those who
of the prophecy, and heed the
which are written in it, for the time is

John to the seven churches
to you and peace from Him who
and who is to come, and from
who are before His throne;
Jesus Christ, the faithful wit
of the dead, and the ruler of
the earth. To Him who loves
us from our sins by His blood,
us to be a kingdom,
God and Father; to Him

over Him. Even so.

9 I, John, your brother and fellow par-
er in the tribulation and kingdom and per-
erance which are in Jesus, was on the island
ed Patmos, because of the word of God
the testimony of Jesus.

I was in the Spirit on the Lord's day,
I heard behind me a loud voice like the
nd of a trumpet,

saying, "Write in a book what you see,
send it to the seven churches: to Ephesus
to Smyrna and to Pergamum and to Thya-

ing to the feet, and gird
with a golden

14 And His head and His hair wer
like white wool, like snow, an
like a flame of fire.

15 and His feet were
bronze, when it has been
furnace, and His voice was like
many waters.

16 And in His right hand He h
stars, and out of His mouth came
edged sword; and His face was
shining in its strength.

17 And when I saw Him
as a dead man. And He laid His righ
upon me,
first and the last,

Living One; and I was

20 As for the mystery of the sev
which you saw
lampstands are the seven churches.

To the angel of the church in E
write:

The One who holds the seven stars
right hand, the One who walks amor
seven golden lampstands, says this:

2 'I know your deeds and your to
perseverance, and that you cannot endu
men, and you put to the test those wh
themselves apostles, and they are not, ar

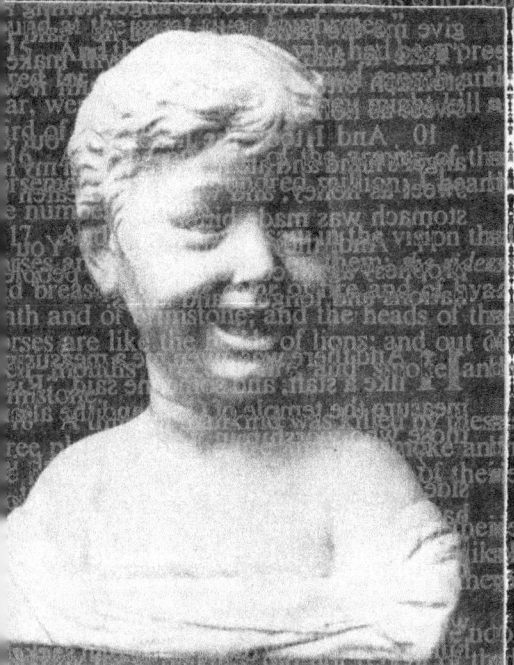

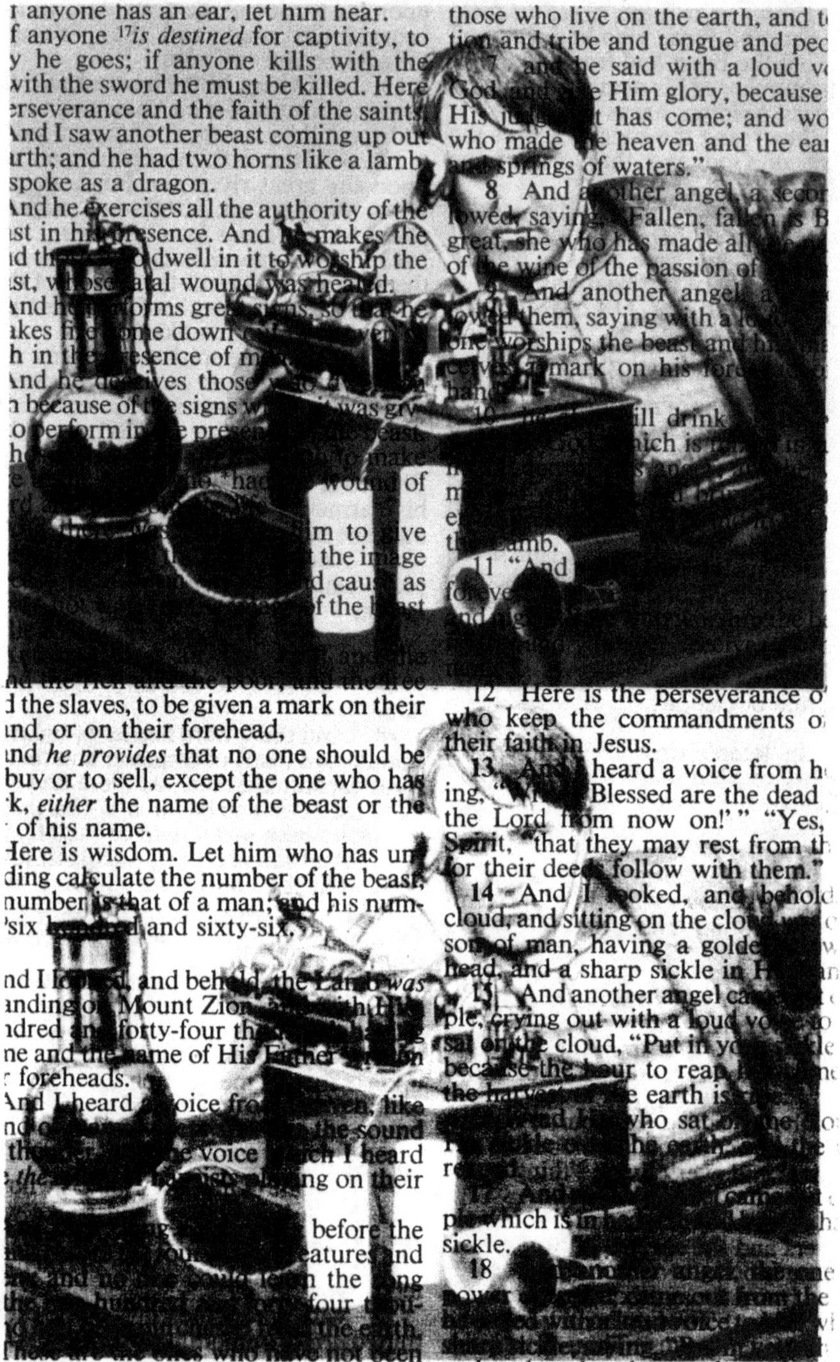

f anyone has an ear, let him hear.
f anyone [17]*is destined* for captivity, to
y he goes; if anyone kills with the
with the sword he must be killed. Here
erseverance and the faith of the saints
And I saw another beast coming up out
rth; and he had two horns like a lamb
spoke as a dragon.
And he exercises all the authority of the
st in his presence. And it makes the
d th... dwell in it to worship the
st, whose... al wound was healed.
And he... worms great signs, so that he
akes fire... down...
h in the... esence of m...
And he deceives those...
h because of the signs w... was giv
o perform in the presen...

those who live on the earth, and t
tion and tribe and tongue and peo
... and he said with a loud v
God... Him glory, because
His ju... has come; and wo
who made... heaven and the ea
... springs of waters."
8   And a... ther angel a secon
lowed, saying... "Fallen, fall... is B
great, she who has made all
of the wine of the passion of
... And another angel a
lowed them, saying with a l
one worships the beast and h
receives... mark on his fo
hand,
... ll drink
... ich is m...
... e
th... amb.
11   "And
for eve...

d the slaves, to be given a mark on their
nd, or on their forehead,
nd *he provides* that no one should be
buy or to sell, except the one who has
k, *either* the name of the beast or the
· of his name.
Here is wisdom. Let him who has un
ding calculate the number of the beast
number is that of a man; and his num-
'six hundred and sixty-six.

nd I looked, and behold, the Lamb *was*
anding on Mount Zion, and with
dred and forty-four th...
ne and the name of His Father wri...
· foreheads.
And I heard a voice from heaven, like
no...
th... voice which I heard
th... ng on their
... before the
... eatures and
... the
... four t...
... the earth.

12   Here is the perseverance o
who keep the commandments o
their faith in Jesus.
13.   And I heard a voice from h
ing, "W... Blessed are the dead
the Lord from now on!'" "Yes,
Spirit, "that they may rest from th
or their deeds follow with them."
14   And I looked, and behold
cloud, and sitting on the clou
son of man, having a golde
head, and a sharp sickle in H
15   And another angel ca
ple, crying out with a loud vo...
sat on the cloud, "Put in yo... le
because the hour to reap...
the harvest... e earth is
... who sat on...
re...
... which is in...
sickle.
18

ABRACADABRA.

אברכאדאברא
אברכאדאבר
אברכאדאב
אברכאדא
אברכאד
אברכא
אברכ
אבר
אב
א

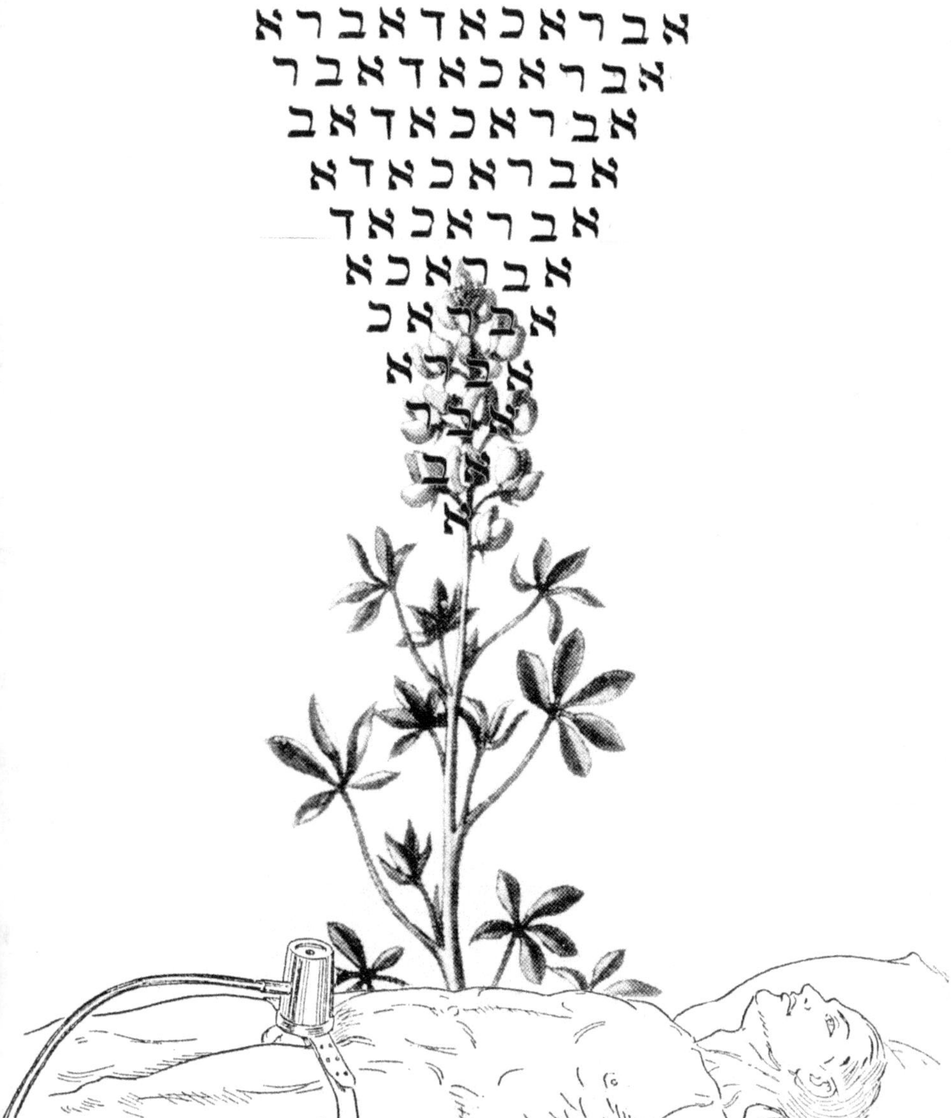

and were crying out as they saw the
ke of her burning, saying, 'What *city* is like

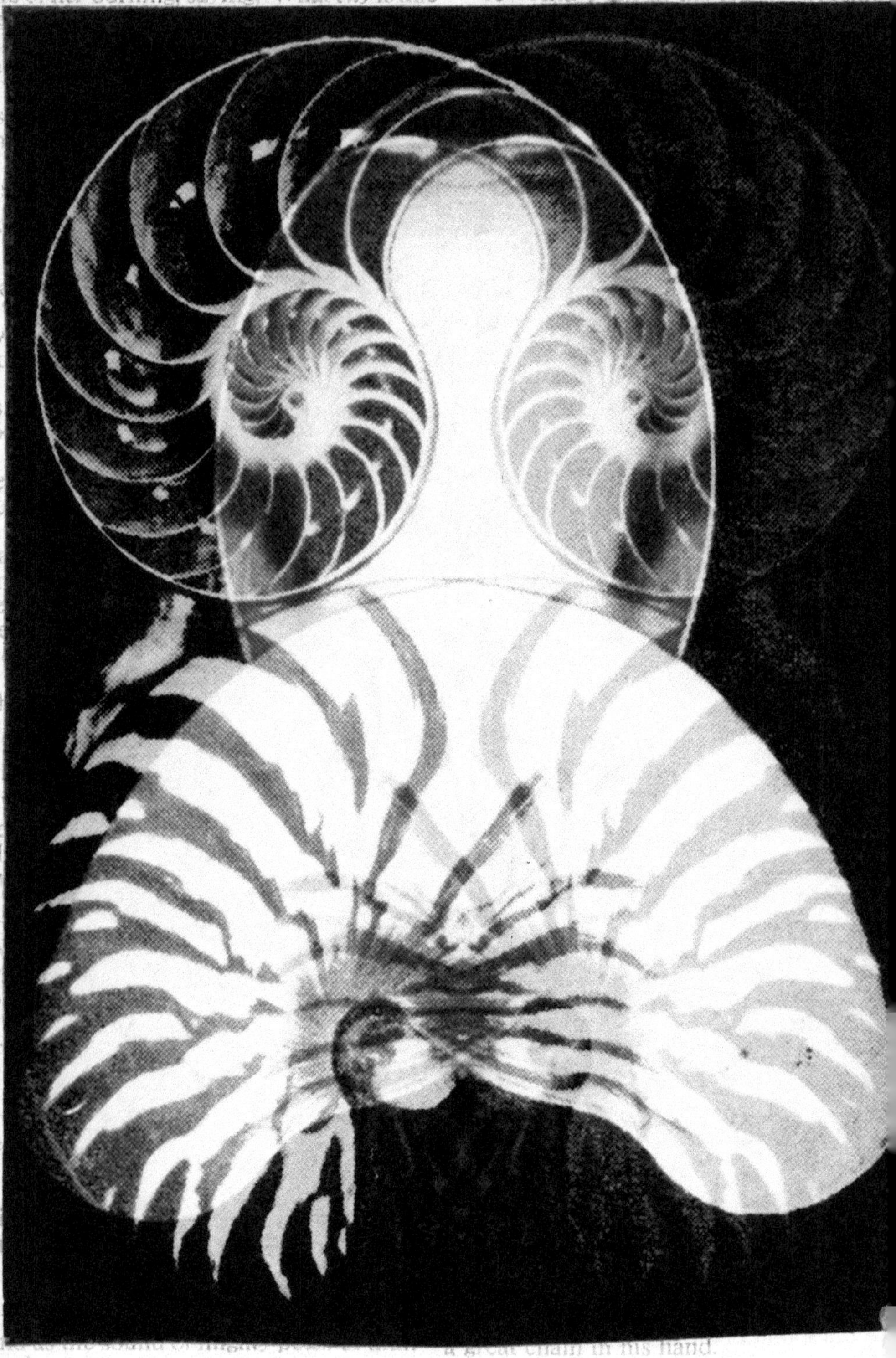

saying,
Hallelujah! For the Lord our God, the Al-
ty, reigns.

"These are true words of God."
10 And I fell at his feet to worship

a great chain in his hand.
2 And he laid hold of the dragon, the
pent of old, who is the devil and Satan,
bound him for a thousand years

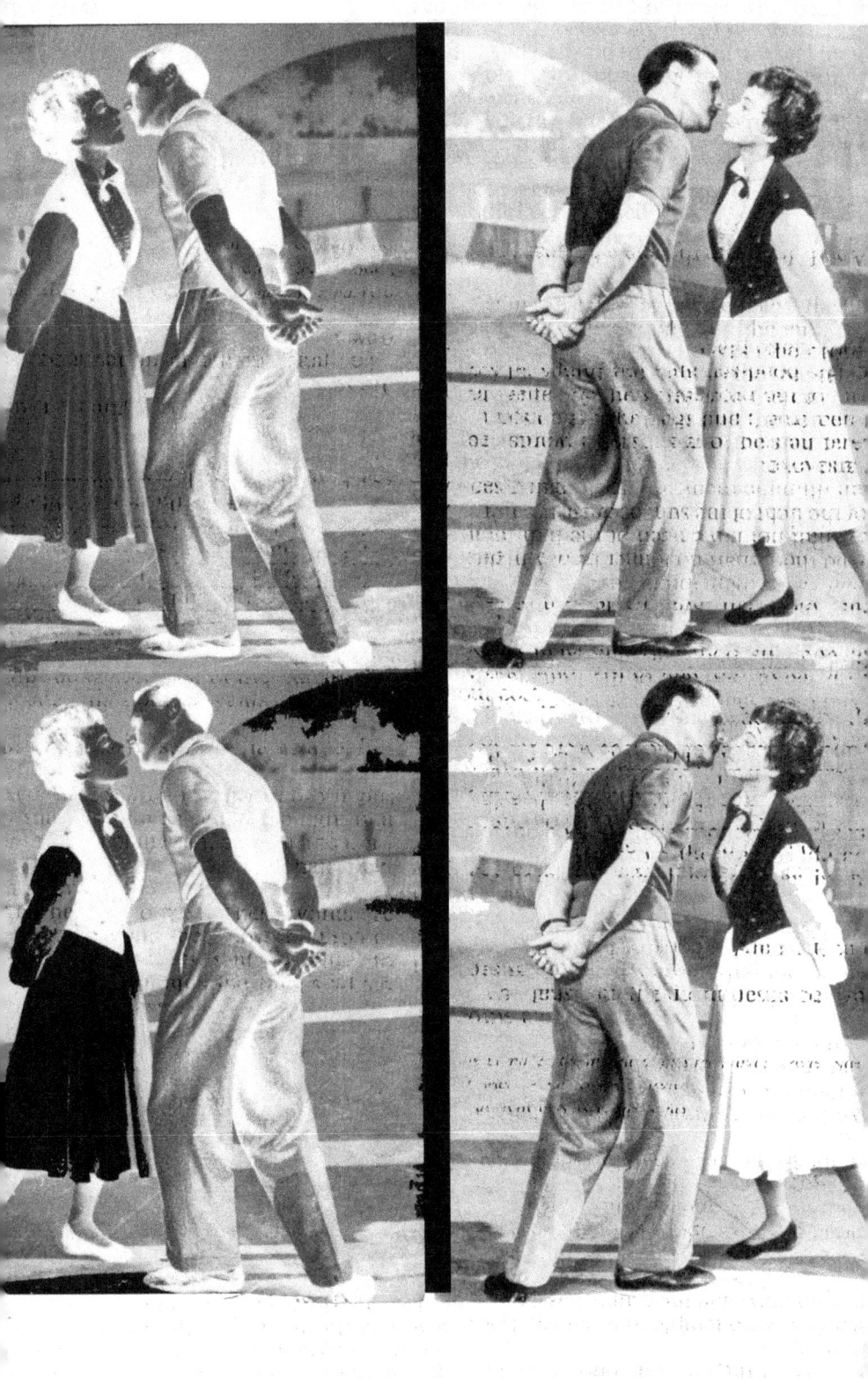

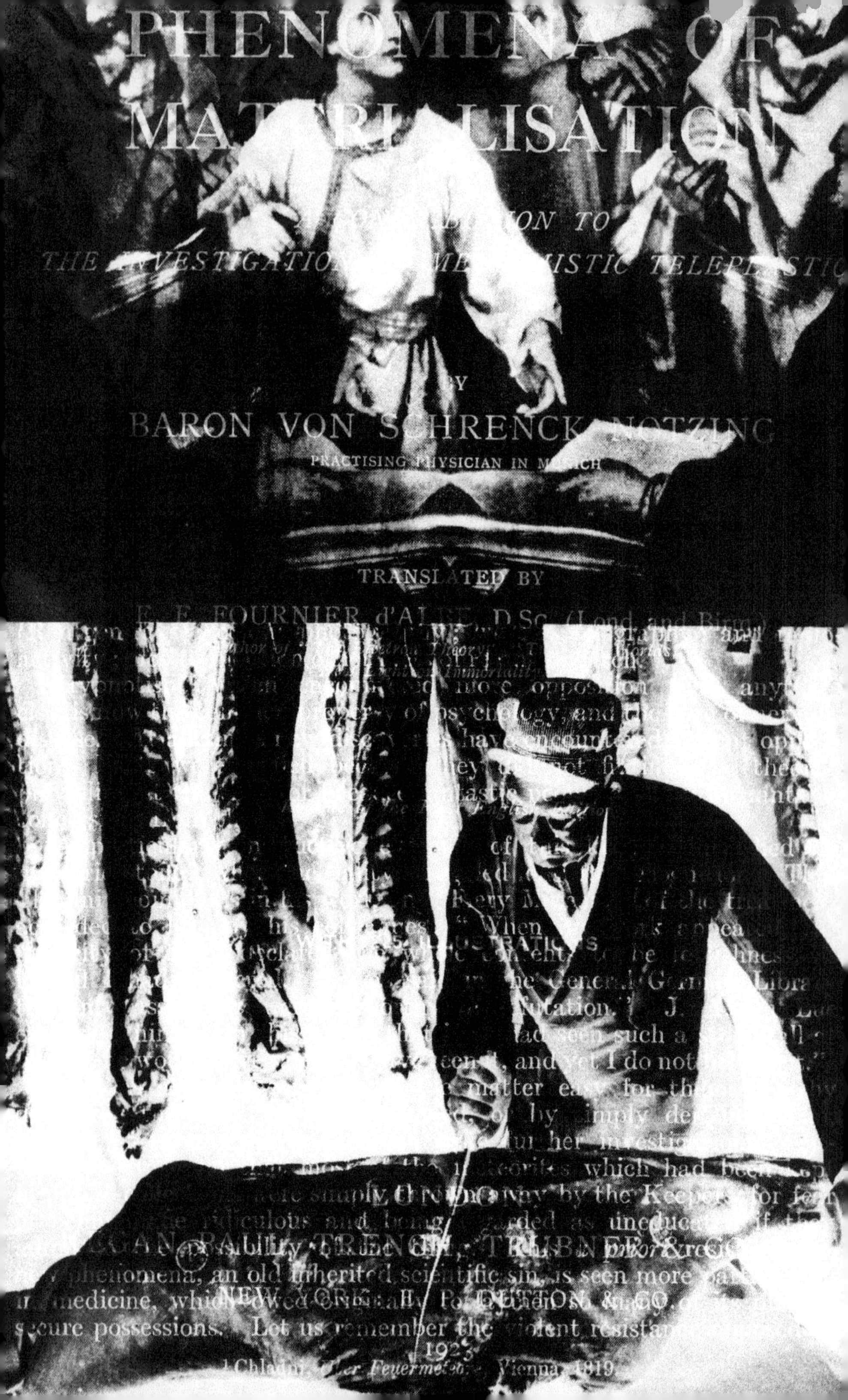

PHENOMENA OF MATERIALISATION

A CONTRIBUTION TO

THE INVESTIGATION OF MEDIUMISTIC TELEPLASTICS

BY

BARON VON SCHRENCK NOTZING

PRACTISING PHYSICIAN IN MUNICH

TRANSLATED BY

E. E. FOURNIER d'ALBE, D.Sc. (Lond. and Birm.)

NEW YORK: E. P. DUTTON & CO.
1923

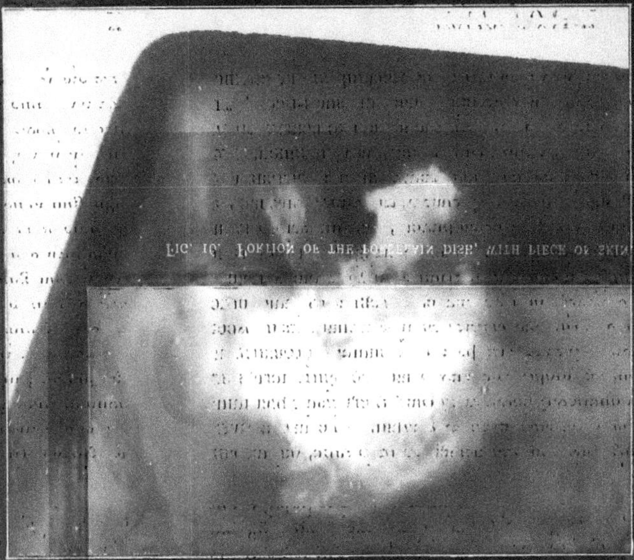

Fig. 16. Portion of the porcelain dish, with piece of skin.

In one of the illustrations

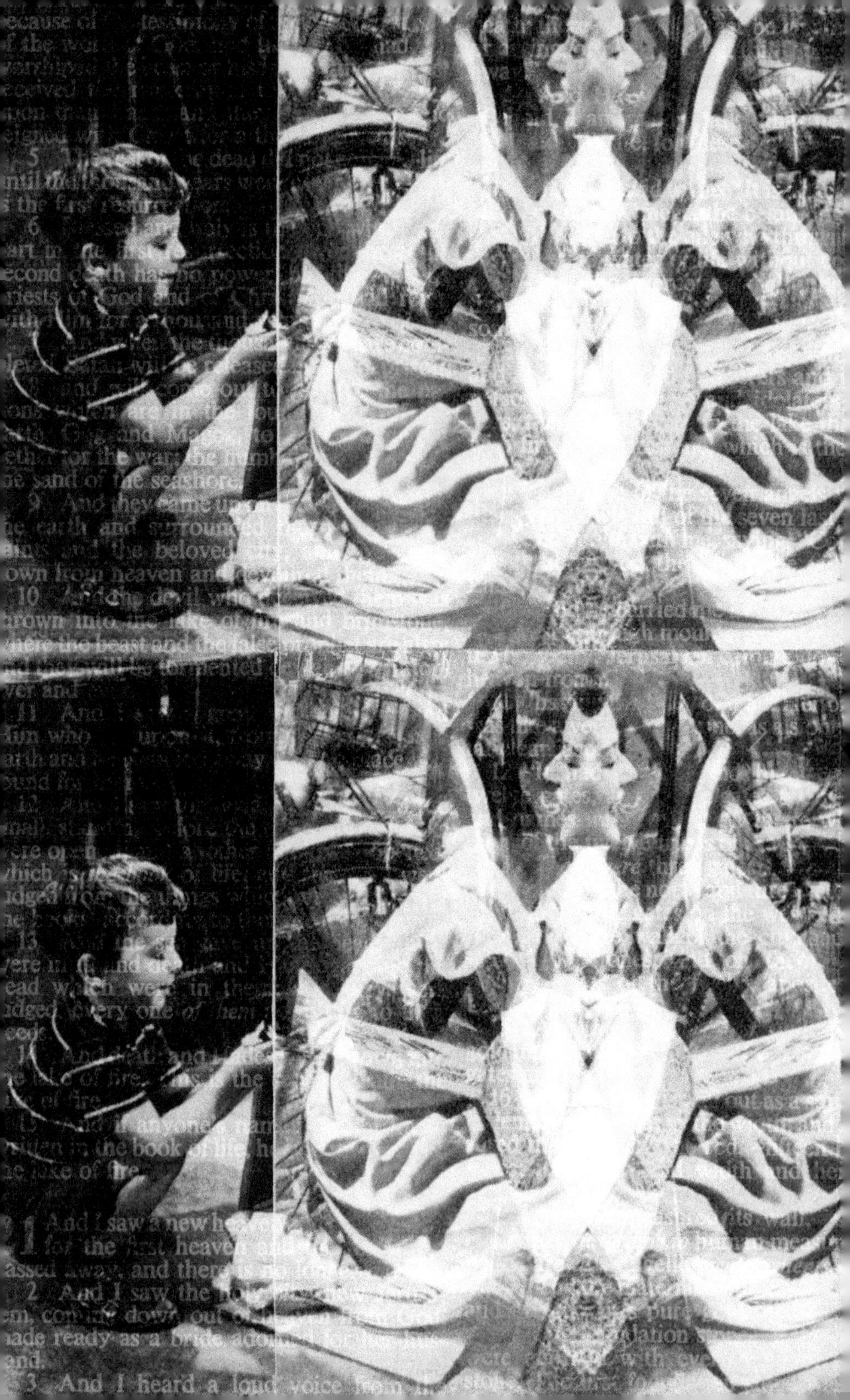
because of the testimony of
5
the first resurrection
6
second death has no power
priests of God and of Christ
the sand of the seashore
9 And they came up
the earth and surrounded
camp of the beloved
down from heaven and
10 And the devil
thrown into the lake of fire and brimstone
where the beast and the false
ever and
11 And
which is the book of life
13
dead which were in them
judged every one of them
the lake of fire
written in the book of life
the lake of fire.
21 And I saw a new heaven
for the first heaven
passed away, and there
2 And I saw the
made ready as a bride adorned
band.
3 And I heard a loud voice from

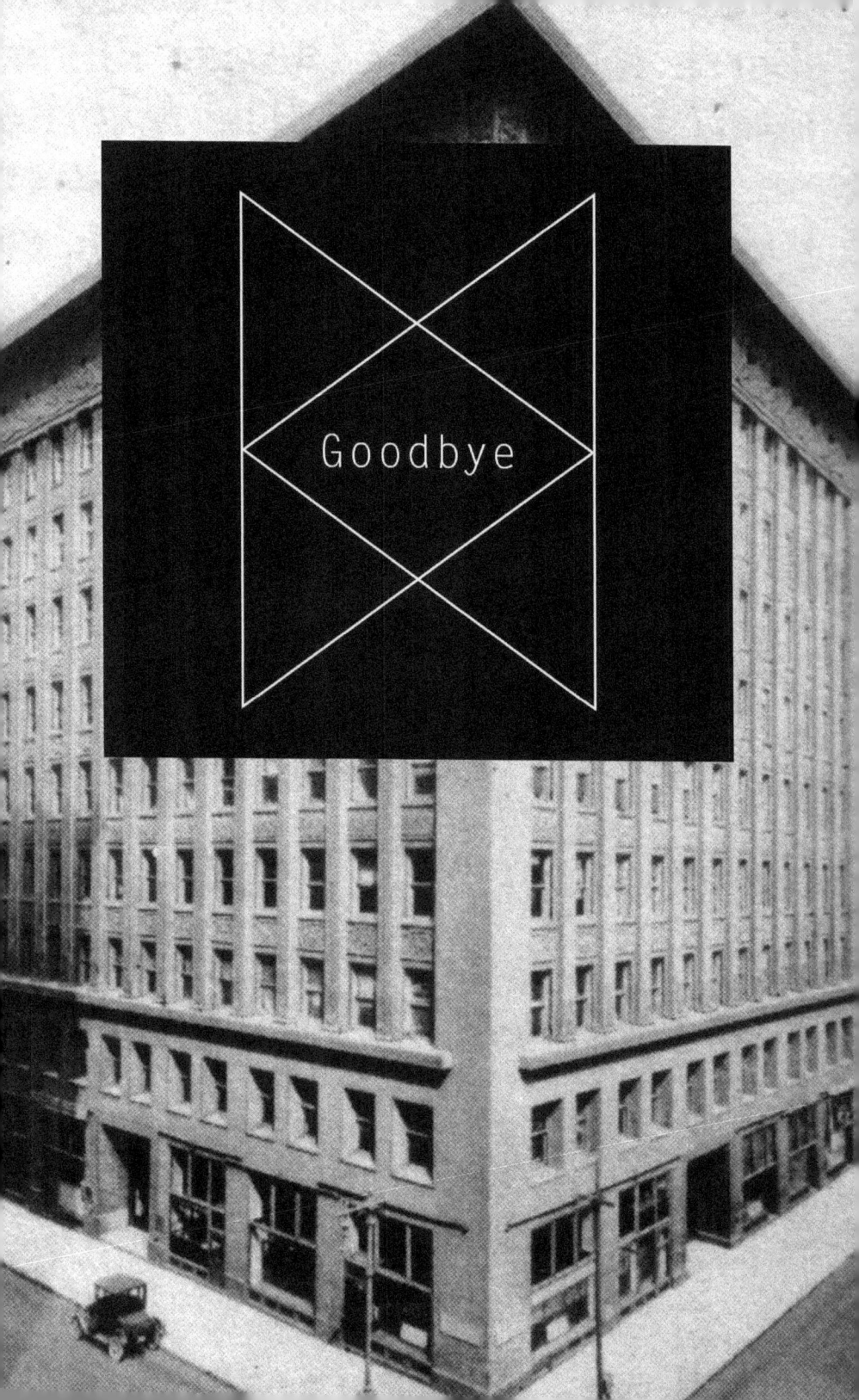

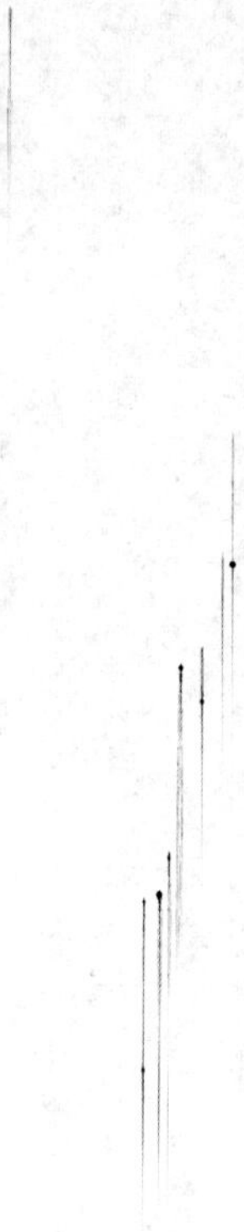

false profit ~ nihil 4
nurturedfutility.com ~ 2015